this is how **yoodoo** it

To Philip,

Thanks for being in
my book!

Best wishes

Mike
Southon

this is how

yoodoo

it.

Great advice from some of the UK's top thinkers on entrepreneurship

65 columns from the *Financial Times* and *Daily Telegraph*, featuring Stephen Fry, Allan Leighton, Brent Hoberman, Kelvin Mackenzie, Peter Jones, Sir Robin Saxby, Sir Keith Mills, Sir Philip Trousdell and many more.

Mike Southon

This is How YooDoo It

First published in 2010 by:

Ecademy Press

48 St Vincent Drive, St Albans, Herts, AL1 5SJ

info@ecademy-press.com

www.ecademy-press.com

Printed and Bound by: Lighning Source in the UK and USA

Set in Trebuchet by Karen Gladwell

Printed on acid-free paper from managed forests. This book is printed on demand, so no copies will be remaindered or pulped.

ISBN: 978-1-905823-98-7

Contents

About The Prince's Trust

The Prince's Trust is a youth charity that helps change young lives.

We address this by giving practical and financial support to the young people who need it most. We work with 14 to 30-year-olds who have struggled at school, have been in care, are long-term unemployed or have been in trouble with the law. We help develop key skills, confidence and motivation, enabling young people to move into work, education or training.

We have helped more than 600,000 young people since 1976 and support 100 more each working day. More than three in four young people we helped last year moved into work, education or training.

We need to raise around £40 million pounds a year to continue our work.

Prince's Trust

this is how **yoodoo** it.

Introduction

Welcome to this is how yoodoo It, a collection of my columns for the *Financial Times* and *Daily Telegraph*

It has been a huge pleasure to write them, as most of them involved meeting fascinating people and learning about the secrets of their success. I have greatly enjoyed getting to know them all, and it is my privilege to pass their knowledge and experience on to readers of this book.

I said 'secrets' (plural) above, as there is rarely just one. However, to make my columns fit the demands of a newspaper audience, I needed to zero in on one aspect of each individual's message. My portraits are thus thumbnail ones rather than intricate Gainsboroughs or Lawrences. But sharper, I hope, as a result.

The book is called this is how yoodoo it, as a nod to our new site, Yoodoo.biz, which has been specifically designed for people thinking of starting a business. You can find more details at the end of the book.

This book is published by Ecademy Press and all proceeds of this book will go to The Prince's Trust, an organisation which embodies the principles and practices featured in this book.

I would like to say a huge thank you to everyone featured in this book. I would also like to thank some very special people who have made it possible.

Chris West has worked with me on all my books since The Beermat Entrepreneur. His name is not on the cover of this one, but he has done his usual excellent editing job on it, turning a set of columns that span several years into a something bigger: a book, a cohesive entity with its own flow and structure.

Jim White mentored me as I made the transition from book author to columnist. Jim is a consummate newspaper professional, and I couldn't have got from there to here without his guidance.

Jonathan Moules has been my editor and mentor at the *Financial Times*, one of the best business brands in the world. I trust him implicitly, giving him free rein to tweak my copy. This includes titles: for example, the column on Stephen Fry and Twitter was originally titled Follow You, Follow Me after the Genesis song. Jonathan changed it to A Wit and to Woo. Pure genius!

I would also like to thank Richard Tyler, who was my editor at the *Daily Telegraph* (another top professional who helped me develop my style) and Nick Saalfeld, who recorded and originally edited the conversations with my subjects for podcast. Without him, I would not have a newspaper column. Finally, many thanks go to Declan Hill and Mike Burge for their meticulous proof-reading.

Business success is all about team building — the people above are all great team players and it's been great (and continues to be great) working with them.

Finally, this book is dedicated to my wife Virginia and son James, for their patience while I tapped away in my office on Sunday mornings, writing these columns.

Mike Southon
Hampstead, October 2010

Part One:

Getting Started

When you set out, the most important thing to get right is yourself: your commitment, your attitudes and your direction.

So I'll begin this selection with some columns on that subject. I begin with a challenge: re-invent yourself! Then a more traditionalist take on starting out: know where you have come from. (Why not try both?) A third piece looks at entrepreneurship as a journey.

I follow this with a piece on what is arguably the most important skill for anyone with a new business. Guy Kawasaki says that the entrepreneur's motto is 'I pitch, therefore I am'. He's right. Your first pitch is to yourself — do I really believe this? Then you are pitching to the world...

I conclude with a piece on starting out as a sole trader. Many entrepreneurs begin this way — and many stay that way, building great businesses and adding value to their customers and the economy in general.

Re-invent Yourself!

Financial Times, 17th November 2007

Bored? Unfulfilled? Then why not just re-invent yourself?

Back in the 80s, Christine Comaford and I were both upstarts in the computer industry; I was opening up an office in Boston for my first start-up, The Instruction Set, while she was working as a contractor at Lotus. Who would have thought, all those years ago, that one day we'd both be best-selling authors?

But we are. Christine's Rules for Renegades is full of expert advice and motivation for entrepreneurs, illustrated by episodes from her own life, including interacting with Bill Gates, Larry Ellison and Hillary Clinton — and a visit to a morgue. One of her key messages is that, as an entrepreneur, you can and should re-invent yourself.

This isn't very British, is it?

Our attitude to failure seems amazingly negative to me. Americans respect you if you try something but fail, while over here, fail once and you're banished, laughed at in the street, or worse.

I met recently with a friend whose last company was wound up, owing money. He picked himself up, dusted himself down and used his skills and contacts to develop another business. As soon as he put his head above the parapet, the hate e-mails started, anonymous of course, implying 'impeding investigations' and asking why anyone would want to do business with this 'crook'.

A few months on, the negative e-mails are drying up and he seems to be doing quite well. Of course he feels for his former creditors, but he set out originally with the best intentions, worked his socks off and never did anything illegal. The bank, in its infinite wisdom, decided suddenly to pull the plug...

He's had to re-invent himself the best he can, and so long as he remains on the right side of the law and does his best, he has my moral support.

Christine admits to making many mistakes — she got mixed up with a false guru, and some ventures failed; she lost several million dollars at one point. But she has also got many things spectacularly right, investing in over 200 start-up businesses, including a small outfit called Google.

Over the years she has founded and sold five of her own companies for an average 700% return on investment. Her group and private mentoring programs at Mighty Ventures enable her clients to regularly triple their value in a year or less. She has now re-invented herself as an author and business mentor, and her book has topped the business best-seller lists in the USA.

I can thoroughly recommend re-inventing yourself; it's tremendous fun. I've variously been a chemical engineer, a computer-training salesman, a spoof rock star, a salesman-for-hire, an author, a professional speaker and now a columnist. I tend to gloss over the adventures that

> "As an entrepreneur, you can and should re-invent yourself"

went terribly wrong, of course, but all the gurus that I meet remind me it's all about the journey, not the destination.

I'm sure many people reading this are thinking about re-inventing themselves as an entrepreneur. The benefits are clear and real, not just dreams: doing something more interesting, being your own boss, generating some serious wealth and making a difference.

Turn your idea into a simple, logical model. Then test this model, getting a small group of people together and looking at the three aspects of the idea: can we deliver the product or service; will it make money if we do; and most crucially, will anyone buy from us in the first place?

The difference between a good idea and a bad idea is that in the former people actually want to buy your 'stuff'. I worked on three start-ups that went broke, essentially because I was unable to sell the 'stuff', however hard I tried. I never really found out if it was my lack of sales skills or the shortcomings of the company; I quickly moved on.

Wise re-invention is usually about taking qualified risks. Can you start quitting your day job or mortgaging your house? If you never even try, you may regret it all of your life. When speaking to groups of entrepreneurs I often quote one of the saddest movie lines of all, from On The Waterfront: "I could have been a contender!"

And if it goes wrong, there's bound to be a useful lesson (or three) from the experience. One of Christine Comaford's less successful ideas was for an American geisha service. It failed. "But I did learn how to make a great cup of tea," she says.

Christine Comaford

New York Times bestselling author of Rules for Renegades, **Christine Comaford** *has built and sold five of her businesses with an average 700% ROI. She is CEO of Mighty Ventures (a business accelerator which massively increases sales, product offerings and company value). She has helped over 150 entrepreneurs to become millionaires.*

www.christine.com

Rules for Renegades **is published by McGraw-Hill**

Three Magic Questions

Financial Times, Saturday 4th October 2008

One of the interesting side effects of the meltdown of international capitalism is a sudden flurry of long-lost contacts sending me business plans.

These former Masters of the Universe are determined to bounce back from the demise of their former employers, and have already generated impressive business plans detailing exactly what they will do next.

However, in my view they are asking the wrong type of question. They shouldn't be asking 'what' questions, but 'who' questions. Three of them, to be precise.

Start with the most basic one of all: 'Who am I?'

They may not realise it, but leaving employment has left these people suddenly short of an identity. Before the crash, they were part of a large and well-respected organisation with a distinctive brand and a long list of things that it stood for. Now, they need to work out what they stand for as individuals.

This is where Ngahihi o te ra (the name means 'rays of the sun') Bidois comes in... He was born to Maori parents in Rotorua, the Maori capital of New Zealand. He was schooled in the traditional European way, took a business degree and worked for a multi-national company. Ultimately, however, he found himself frustrated and unfulfilled, and decided to re-connect with his traditional culture. To do this properly, he learnt, he would have to have his face tattooed with the traditional 'Ta Moko'.

Eight hours under the needle turned out to be a profoundly spiritual experience. It was the start of a new part of his journey of self-discovery, which now sees Ngahihi delivering leadership courses to business people, based on traditional Maori wisdom.

Eight hours of face tattooing may not be right for every aspirant entrepreneur — but the process of re-discovering yourself and establishing your own brand can be just as radical and life changing.

My first advice for the newly unemployed is to take a holiday: however resilient you are, you have been damaged by the experience and need some time to reconnect with yourself and your family.

But I then suggest a slightly unusual step: undertake a little genealogy. Ngahihi discovered a strong connection with his ancestors, and was able to re-channel that almost genetic experience into his modern life. Even if you just have a chat with your parents and grandparents about their life, it will help you to put any current misfortunes into perspective. We sometimes forget we are all only a generation or two away from the tramp of jackboots, war and years of rationing.

> "The process of re-discovering yourself and establishing your own brand can be radical and life-changing"

Once you have developed a sense of perspective, your second 'who' question to ask is 'who do I plan to work with?' Your identity is also defined by the people you can attract to work with you. They should have complementary skills to your own: if you are extrovert, they should be introvert; if you are good at starting projects, they should be good at finishing them; if you are bad with money, they should be good with it.

A complete start-up team has just three people, covering delivery, sales and finance. Ngahihi tells me that tribal society is very similar, with people naturally falling into specific roles of farming, hunting and organisation.

When you start a new business, you start a new tribe. A key element of a successful tribe is everyone knowing their place and respecting everyone else's expertise. A poor entrepreneur, like a poor middle manager, is someone who ignores this and feels the need to meddle.

The third and final 'who' question is 'who are you going to sell to?' Most successful entrepreneurs sell first to people they know, so your personal network should also contain your first potential customers, people who know and trust you and are willing to give your new business a chance.

It is a big moment when you go into your first sales visit, and it is wise to have a list of questions you need to ask and benefits you can explain. Ngahihi has a built-in checklist, which he sees in the mirror every morning. The design of his tattoos explains that he should look first, then listen, then think, and only then finally talk — more excellent advice for any new entrepreneur.

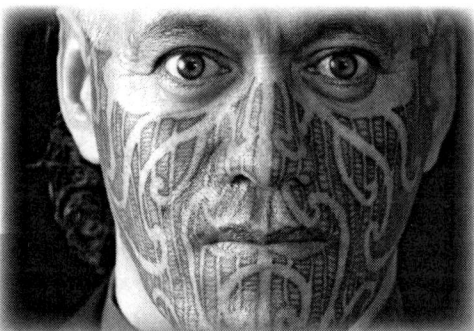

Ngahihi o te ra Bidois

Ngahihi o te ra Bidois is an International Speaker and Consultant. He is the National Speakers Association New Zealand (Auckland) 2008 Speaker of the Year and Inspirational Speaker of the Year. His Inspirational Leadership keynote speeches, MC services and Seminars are presented in New Zealand, England, Asia and Australia.

www.ngahibidois.com

The Hero's Journey

Financial Times, 6th September 2008

I hear dozens of new business ideas every week, and
they all have some merit.

The real challenge is making sure that the entrepreneur has 'the
right stuff'.

This is a theme developed by entrepreneur, coach and NLP
trainer Robbie Steinhouse, in his book Think Like an Entrepreneur.
It mixes Robbie's business experience with his knowledge of
psychological systems such as Neuro Linguistic Programming (NLP)
and Transactional Analysis (TA).

Robbie uses a simple metaphor for entrepreneurship, one that has
been popular in storytelling since ancient times: a hero's journey.
Entrepreneurship is seen as a quest that goes through various stages.
First, there is a calling, which the hero has to accept.

They then have to pass some real or imagined threshold. They will
enlist the help of some guardians with special knowledge or powers
before they fight the dreaded demon. Finally, the hero reaches their
goal and brings home their rewards to universal acclaim.

Demons come in many forms but not all of them are external.
When coaching entrepreneurs, Robbie spends much of his time
addressing inner demons. He has encountered many entrepreneurs
who have snatched defeat from the jaws of victory.

There is always a psychological reason for this. NLP explains that
every negative character trait has a 'positive intention' — in other
words at some time in the past, the trait was (or appeared to be)
of benefit. This benefit must now be detached from the trait and
given a realistic, up-to-date alternative expression. The book shows
how to do this, as well as including some intriguing examples.

Robbie also has a useful tool called the 'permission pattern',
which you can use to overcome psychological barriers, which are
preventing you from starting your own business. Such barriers are

common among people who come from an authoritarian family or tradition, or have spent a long time working for a large organisation where they have been conditioned to take, rather than give orders.

Experienced corporate people also often spend far too much time analysing the market before making the big leap into entrepreneurship. This was the way they did

"Just go out and get a first customer"

things in their large company, and makes total sense in that environment, but Robbie contends that to establish a new business you have to bypass most of that process and just go out and get a first customer.

This replicates the best behaviour of most successful entrepreneurs who originally got started by simply getting off their backsides and making a sale, even if their products or services were not quite ready. The book contains excellent tools for how to establish rapport ▶

Robbie Steinhouse

A successful serial entrepreneur, Robbie Steinhouse was running his own market stall by his early teens, and also spent time as a drummer in a rock band and travelling the world before building his property and insurance group, Gray's Inn Estates, into a highly successful enterprise managing over 40,000 properties in the UK.

Robbie now concentrates on the human side of business as a trainer and coach, using tools from NLP, Transactional Analysis and coaching, and works with enterprises ranging from large corporations to solo entrepreneurs.

More details:
www.nlpschool.com &
www.coachingconsultancy.co.uk

Think Like an Entrepreneur is
published by Prentice Hall

quickly in these crucial sales meetings by the clever use of body language and good listening techniques.

Robbie attributes his own success to building a team of 'guardians', professional people such as accountants, lawyers and other successful business people who can always spare ten minutes on the phone to help him on his journey. Get Merlin, Gandalf and Yoda on your side!

If you defeat the demon out there — or inside you — you will return in triumph with the fruits of your success. You do not want to end up instead like another character mentioned in the book: Sisyphus. He was cursed with always having to push the same boulder uphill, perhaps the perfect analogy of the corporate job you might be thinking of leaving to run your own business.

Perfect Pitch

Financial Times, 14th March 2009

One of the most enjoyable parts of my work is appearing at elevator pitch competitions, where hopeful entrepreneurs extol the virtues of their business ideas.

These events are both joyous and frustrating at the same time; there is nothing more joyous than listening to entrepreneurs explaining how they are going to change the world. What is frustrating is that few people have worked out how to pitch their ideas in a simple form.

Yet there is plenty of material around about how to do this. My own book The Beermat Entrepreneur, for example, or a book by Chris O'Leary, called Elevator Pitch Essentials.

The first thing to note about elevator pitches is that that your elevator should not get stuck for several hours; keep your pitch short and simple. The worst culprits here are inventors, engineers and technologists who feel that they have to cram as many features as possible into their pitch.

In sales, there is the well-known concept of 'golden nuggets', the amazing features of your product that have been lovingly crafted into product literature by your marketing team. The problem is that most customers have very short attention spans and can only remember three things about your product.

As soon as you mention the fourth 'golden nugget' the first and probably most important one drops out of their active memory. By the time you get to nugget number 50 all the most compelling ones have long since gone. The prospective customer has also lost the will to live.

The objective in delivering an elevator pitch is not to secure an order there and then; the best you can hope for is to stimulate enough interest for them to give you another 15 minutes and to hand over their business card. The methodology for a good elevator pitch is very simple, and centres around five Ps: pain, premise, people, proof and purpose.

The most important question for any would-be entrepreneur is "where's the pain?" The larger the pain, the more likely people are to give you money to take it away. Pain can come in many forms, but if your product or service saves time and money that is a very good start.

Next you have to explain in simple terms the premise of your business, exactly what you do. For this, you need to be precise and not descend into sloganeering. "We transform people's lives" is laudable but impossibly vague. "We are a bespoke training company, specialising in communication skills" is much more to the point.

> "The larger the pain, the more likely people are to give you money to take it away"

You think this is obvious? Visit a trade show and try and work out what each company does, just from the text on their display stands. Half the time, you won't be able to. Some are being deliberately unclear in the hope your curiosity will be aroused; others just don't realize they are being obscure.

You need to talk about your people, as entrepreneurship is a team game. Investors say they look for a credible team rather than a good idea, and customers say they buy from people not companies.

Proof is the hardest to provide: why anyone should buy from you and not your competitors. Even if you have the best team and products in the world, people can still be sceptical. The best proof is examples of your happy customers, in the form of case studies.

The final P is purpose. Of course, the most important purpose of any business is to make money. Potential investors will be looking for a return on their investment, and prospective customers will want to know that you run a sensible and profitable business, so they can be sure of reliable and consistent delivery of your products and services. But more and more I am finding that entrepreneurs want some social purpose to their business too.

Take time over your pitch. Don't be afraid to amend it as circumstances change. And I look forward to hearing it next time I'm at one of those competitions.

Chris O'Leary

Chris O'Leary is a writer, speaker, consultant and general expert in the fields of innovation, entrepreneurship, new product development, sales and marketing. Chris has contributed to the success of a number of successful start-up companies including SalesLogix, who are makers of the leading middle-market Customer Relationship Management (CRM) application.

www.elevatorpitchessentials.com

A Safe Pair of Hands

Financial Times, 22nd March 2008

Gordon Brown once said his ambition was to be seen as 'a safe pair of hands'.

We will see if history will finally judge him so, but if I want to find safe hands I look away from Westminster and concentrate instead at the millions of 'sole traders' around me, a group of people for whom this term could have been invented.

Sole traders are often overlooked in discussions about entrepreneurship, which generally focus on growing the business, hiring more people and looking for a suitable exit. But these people are an essential part of the economy.

The career path of the sole trader often follows a well-trodden route. They generally spend their twenties learning their craft working for someone else. In their thirties, they have found their niche and have built up a client base of people willing to hire them directly, rather than from the company they work for. This can be doing anything from high-powered consulting to fixing the boiler.

Some take on other people and grow their businesses, but many prefer to work just for themselves, using trusted associates when they need to deliver large projects.

Ian Sanders has written a book about his experiences as a sole trader, called LEAP! Ditch Your Job, Start Your Own Business & Set Yourself Free. The title sums up perfectly the allure of being self-employed: freedom; an end to boredom; the ability to make a real difference, both to yourself and to the people around you.

But freedom brings with it insecurity; working for yourself is a lonely and often terrifying prospect. As a consequence, much of his book is focused on providing the motivation to 'go for it' in the first place.

The prospective sole trader has to understand that they will have to do all three jobs in business: sales, delivery and finance.

this is how **yoodoo** it.

Delivery is not usually a problem; the sole trader has to be good at something. In Ian's case it was about delivering large projects for Unique Broadcasting, a media company founded by Noel Edmonds. These projects spanned radio production, live events and providing broadcast facilities. They involved a heady mix of demanding clients, challenging briefs, broad disciplines, tough deadlines and the inevitable hurdles along the way. Ian learned how to cope with extreme pressure and still deliver on time and to budget.

Finance does not have to be an issue, either. Your first hire should be a good bookkeeper, probably on a part-time basis in the early days.

The real challenge is sales. Many people find the actual process of selling very uncomfortable.

But the successful sole trader knows they need to be selling

> "The prospective sole trader has to understand that they will have to do all three jobs in business: sales, delivery and finance"

all the time. This is not insensitively launching into a sales pitch to everyone they meet, but always making sure they are mixing socially with potential customers and telling interesting and relevant stories of customer problems they have solved.

Ideally, selling is not just about finding pieces of business; it is also about generating a consistent pipeline of work. But even in good times, this is hard to do. Sole traders have to learn to live with this: Ian says his sales pipeline is rarely more than three months full. He remains confident that something will turn up — and it nearly always does.

So being self-employed is not for the faint-hearted. In my Sales on a Beermat workshop I explain that the process is essentially very simple. First, you need to find people with problems and money. Then, you get them to like you, in the first instance by being nice (easy to deal with), local (just around the corner or otherwise easily accessible) and reliable (you deliver on your promises).

If you fulfil these three criteria, happy customers will tell all their friends, generating referral business. The world will then beat a path to your door — or, if you are a politician, they will re-elect you. This is because, like Ian Sanders, you are indeed considered as 'a safe pair of hands'.

Ian Sanders

Ian Sanders is a project-manager, ideas-producer, writer and marketing consultant. He runs a business and marketing consultancy, OHM, whose clients range from huge corporations to one-person start-ups. He is author of two business books: Leap! and, most recently, Juggle! He has also just co-produced a new book for children.

www.iansanders.com

LEAP! Ditch Your Job, Start Your Own Business & Set Yourself Free is published by Capstone.

Part Two:

Sales

Nobody who knows me will be surprised that this is the next topic of this anthology!

I believe profoundly that the most important skill in a start-up is sales. If you have no sales, you have no business, however wonderful your product, marketing plans, wealthy backers or whatever.

The best place to start in sales is with the right attitude to your customers, so I begin with a couple of pieces on this topic. Then I talk about networking and getting referrals.

I introduce a powerful sales tool I have invented myself, my 'Magic E-mail'. There are pieces on tendering — for this one I went right to the top, and spoke to the man who'd run the London 2012 Olympic Bid — and the business of getting everyone in your company involved in sales.

I conclude the section with a couple of pieces on negotiation and deal-making, something that sales people are often surprisingly poor at.

Love your Customers

Financial Times, 3rd May 2008

When I run sales workshops I always test the temperature of the audience by asking about their favourite customer.

This is not necessarily the biggest one, but the one that they like most on a personal level. This is to help me to get a feel for their business and how they deliver their products or services, and to help them replicate their best practices, based on successful customer case studies.

Occasionally some members of the audience look at me blankly and further probing reveals that they actually can't stand their customers: difficult people, who always seem to be complaining and constantly looking for lower prices.

At this point I feel they are in need of counselling as well as sales coaching. I can't help with counselling, but if they want to learn about taking a more positive attitude to their customers, they should speak to Richard Richardson.

Richard had a very successful career in advertising, ending up at Young and Rubicam. His favourite customer was John Barnes at Kentucky Fried Chicken, and the two of them used to spend many hours cooking up new business ideas, just for fun.

> "They share common values: a love of customers and the business of day-to-day interaction with them"

But one idea appealed so much that they felt they had to take it somewhere: what about the original British fast food, fish and chips? The best-known name, Harry Ramsden's, was a single large restaurant at Guiseley in Yorkshire, plus a few other outlets, differently branded. The owners were looking to sell, and John and Richard saw the opportunity to build a great brand, something they were both passionate about.

this is how **yoodoo** it.

John and Richard are a great double act, with very complementary skills; John is the charismatic ideas man, Richard the completer/finisher. But they share common values, one of which is a love of customers and of the business of day-to-day interaction with customers.

They raised some money and then set about building the Harry Ramsden's brand, but without the large marketing budgets they were both used to. They developed a style, which they later captured in their book Marketing Judo.

Most important of all, they instilled a sense of customer awareness in their team by insisting that everyone in the 25-person head office called at least five unhappy customers every week — including the bosses.

This caused some bemusement amongst their customers, particularly a gentleman who had filled in a card to complain about some cold chips at their Bournemouth outlet. He

Richard Richardson

Richard Richardson began his career in marketing and advertising before joining John Barnes in the acquisition of Harry Ramsden's, turning it from a single restaurant into an international brand.

He is co-author with John Barnes of the best-selling business book, **'Marketing Judo'** (published by Prentice Hall) *and is a frequent speaker at conferences.*

was so surprised to hear from a director of the company that he dropped his phone.

The customer then explained that he had just bought a car for £35,000 and was having a lot less joy in having problems resolved with the car than with his 70p bag of chips. He also said that he regularly received parties of visiting Chinese business people, and in future would take them to Harry Ramsden's.

Being close to your customers means you can also create successful new products. John and Richard cite many examples of how they have done this. The Glasgow branch offered haggis, and they created an all-in package for senior citizens on a coach trip followed by a Harry Ramsden's fish supper. They call this 'getting the crowd on your side'.

If you do this, not only will you grow to love your customers, you will find they will love you right back, and do your marketing for you, by word of mouth.

Wow!

Financial Times, 12th January 2008

So when was the last time you said 'Wow!" about the quality of customer service you received?

My guess is you are thinking the exact opposite, especially during the holiday break, when civilization in the UK seems to grind to a complete halt. Perhaps you were fuming at the state of the rail network; perhaps, like me, you are waiting for your dentist to amble back to work somewhere around the second week in January; you might even still be trying to arrange delivery of some Christmas presents ordered over the internet.

You have two alternatives in the face of this. One is to slump into a Victor Meldrew-like state of resigned desperation and look for an alternative supplier. The other is to consider the glass to be half full, learn from these appalling examples of customer service and do the opposite: put the 'Wow!' back into your existing business. You can even do this if you are just an employee. It may not make you rich, but you'll have a lot more fun.

> "However big your company, people buy from people"

This is the manifesto of the inimitable Paul Dunn, a serially successful entrepreneur. Paul has tried to retire several times but cannot seem to stop himself getting involved in new and interesting things. He is much in demand as a speaker, and focuses on getting people and organisations to improve their products and services so that at the end of the experience the customer says "Wow!"

This is far too important to leave just in the hands of your marketing department. However big your company, people buy from people. They also stop buying from rude and aggressive people: customer service problems tend to stem from individual members of staff with negative attitudes rather than flaws in abstract marketing processes. So you must get these individuals trained up.

Paul Dunn

Paul Dunn began his career in Australia at Hewlett Packard and then wrote some innovative software that became the basis for one of Australia's early technological successes, Hartley Computer. He later formed Results Accountants' Systems (RAS), teaching them to leverage their skills to create far better businesses for their clients. He now owns successful businesses around the world and is passionate about giving back to social causes, serving as Chairman of the revolutionary Buy1GIVE1 organisation, connecting business, charities and customers.

www.B1G1.com

Much more common, however, are people who are fantastic at customer service, but buried below layers of management so nobody actually sees the great things they are doing. Treasure these people; learn from them; they will show you how to improve your 'Wow!' factor.

When I give workshops in large companies instilling the entrepreneurial mindset, 'Wow!' ideas soon start flowing. These come from everybody, not just the extroverts. The best ideas often come from the quiet ones who observe, reflect and consider before making their contribution.

In larger companies there is always a paradox.

A structured organisation requires processes and rules, and these are the natural enemies of innovation. Common complaints are "nobody actually listens to us" and "we can't make a difference".

In small companies (which we define in our Beermat model to be less than 20 employees) this is rarely a problem. The tribal nature of the organisation lends itself to regular social gatherings, where all sorts of ideas are kicked around. The skill of the entrepreneur lies in choosing which ones really have commercial magic and which ones just sound good.

I asked Paul about his own current personal 'Wow!' It's a very simple concept: 'Buy One, GIVE One Free'. What if every time a Plasma TV was sold, a blind person got the gift of sight? What if every time a book was sold, a tree was planted? What if every time someone dined out, a hungry kid was fed?

Paul Dunn is applying a social purpose to consumerism, and everybody wins. Wow!

Connecting is not Enough

Financial Times, 25th July 2009

It is often said that your personal value is not what you know, but whom you know.

This is powerful motivation for recent graduates to build their personal networks. Those of us of a certain age may have concluded that we already have enough friends and contacts; our challenge is making the best use of those that we already have.

The mathematics supports this argument. If you have been in business for over 20 years, you probably have more than 150 close contacts, defined as people you like and respect and would recognise if you bumped into them out of their normal work context.

If you add to this all the people in their close networks, this aggregates to potentially more than 20,000 agreeable and interesting people. On top of this, we have networking prospects; a drawer full of business cards and often a large number of on-line connections.

So it's not network-building that is the problem, but getting the best out of the network we already have: how do we fully 'leverage' our existing contacts without appearing sleazy and manipulative?

The most important lesson to learn from the best-connected individuals is that little of their networking activity is carried out with any specific business goal in mind. They concentrate their effort on people they most like and who seem to like them right back.

Even for the shyest individual, all that is required to leverage their network is to generate a list of people whose company they have enjoyed over the years and invite them to a private dinner. This would be apropos of nothing in particular other than the pleasure of good company and an opportunity for their friends to meet other interesting people.

The tools for engineering a mutually successful outcome of such events are well explained by one of Europe's leading business networking strategists, Andy Lopata. His site explains that connecting is not enough; it is important also to determine how well your contacts understand what you do and then how inspired they might be to provide a referral.

Andy provides in-depth networking training and coaching and is always amazed to discover how few companies have an effective referral strategy. One investment bank merely had a system for asking for two referrals at the end of every meeting, regardless of whether they had actually built up any trust with the client.

Andy explains that the chances of receiving a referral are greatly increased if the potential referrer trusts you and understands exactly what you do: how you help people and the problems you solve.

Everyone understands that we are all fundamentally in business to generate profits for our companies and in the process earn a decent living, but your chances of receiving a referral are greatly increased if you are also perceived to have a wider purpose to your working life.

> They concentrate their effort on people they most like and who seem to like them right back

This may not be as noble and altruistic as working for a social enterprise solving problems in the developing world, but you should at least demonstrate how you can make the process of business in general more fun and interesting by your own personal efforts.

Andy recommends making a detailed assessment of your best contacts; the people they know, their willingness to refer you to them and how exactly you might inspire them to make that valued introduction, for free.

While some people offer direct financial rewards for referrals, seasoned networkers mostly make introductions on the basis that everyone gains real benefits, including the prospect of referrals in return.

Although high-level networking is primarily a face-to-face activity, Andy agrees that on-line tools greatly accelerate the process. LinkedIn is probably the best tailored for this purpose; you can connect with people you know, like and trust, and you can also search specifically for long-lost colleagues from former companies whom you remember as being fun and interesting.

If you explain yourself and your purpose well, the people you connect with should happily provide referrals to their best contacts, primarily on the basis that both of you would enjoy meeting each other; any subsequent business would represent a bonus, rather than the prime objective.

Expert networkers like Andy work on the basis that if you connect with your network on this mutually beneficial basis, the financial rewards will definitely flow. The old formula of 'who you know' is not enough. The true value of your network is whom you know and what these people say about you.

Successful networking should be genuinely selfless and altruistic, always giving referrals without remembering your simple favour, and receiving them without forgetting their kind gift.

Andy Lopata

Andy Lopata is former Managing Director of UK network Business Referral Exchange and co-author of two books on networking.

He works with companies from one-man bands to global organisations to help them realise the full potential from their networking.

He is also a former vice-president of the Professional Speakers Association.

www.lopata.co.uk

Mike's Magic E-Mail

Financial Times, 18th April 2009

I recently returned from speaking in the Far East to an in-box of several hundred e-mails.

Many hoped to interest me in their services or suggest subjects for this column. Almost all had one major drawback; they were far too long.

There is a saying attributed to many, including Mark Twain: "I am sorry to write you a long letter, I did not have time to send a short one." We all send too many e-mails and most of them are far too verbose. The attention span of a potential customer is very short, so you need to convey a very simple message with a clear call to action.

A common mistake is to attempt to convey complex philosophies, deep emotions or humour in an e-mail; this can go horribly wrong. It is very important to realise that e-mail is a very inefficient form of communication for anything other than basic facts. It should always ask a very obvious question designed to elicit a simple 'yes' or 'no'.

> You need to convey a very simple message with a clear call to action

When used correctly, e-mail can be very effective and take the misery out of making appointments with customers — a particular problem as most business prospects now hide behind voice-mail.

'Mike's Magic E-Mail' is only four lines long, and has the first benefit of applying discipline to the writer, including basic marketing to define first precisely who it is you are targeting and exactly what it is you are trying to sell them.

Start by looking at your existing happy customers, studying their profile, including company type, location and size. Then go out and assemble a good set of target companies similar to your favourite customers. Then employ a telemarketing company to secure the right contact names and e-mail addresses at these companies. Finally you have to employ the gifts and discipline of Mark Twain to write these people an e-mail that is only four lines long.

The first line should address the pain, problem or challenge that the customer faces, based on your research or market knowledge. Sometimes you have little information on a particular prospect, but a visit to the 'news' or 'press' pages of their website will generate some ideas.

The second line explains the premise of your business: how you plan to help them with their pain. It is important to be specific here, avoiding slogans or by-lines generated by your marketing agency. You may indeed be achieving 'vorsprung durch technik', but you actually need to explain here that you provide reliable and cost-effective cars.

In the third line you back up the bold claim in your premise. The best proof is always an example customer. You should have a one-line customer endorsement backed up by a web link to a full case study on your website.

The fourth and final line is your call to action. Be bold: request a 15-minute meeting on a specific date, as you 'happen to be in the area' (as salespeople often mysteriously are).

So if your ambition is to be featured in this column, your 'Magic E-Mail' might read:

"Dear Mike, I see you are interested in meeting interesting people who might have useful learning points for your readers. We represent Jane Smith, one of the UK's leading entrepreneurs. She has successfully grown her business in a recession using simple but very effective sales techniques. Are you free at 10am on Tuesday 28th to meet her over a coffee?"

Now that sounds interesting!

A free downloadable PDF of my Magic E-mail can be found on http://tinyurl.com/Mikes-Magic-Email

Tendering

Financial Times, 24th November 2007

If you're currently tendering for some major work, here's a top tip: get Nelson Mandela to endorse your bid.

This certainly helped the London 2012 Olympics. Of course, most of us aren't that well connected. But there is a serious point here: for the bid you hope to win, who is your Nelson Mandela, the high-profile individual who would add significant credibility to your offering?

I was talking about London 2012 with Sir Keith Mills, who led the bid team. After a successful career in advertising, he originated the idea of Air Miles, forming the Loyalty Management Group which runs the highly successful Nectar and other customer loyalty programmes.

> Companies can go bankrupt gearing up for a big pitch they have little chance of winning

Then he ran the 2012 bid. He is currently building Team Origin, the UK team for the America's Cup — one of the world's oldest sporting competitions, and one that, sadly, Britain has never won. Yet Sir Keith's bidding experience has many useful lessons for anyone involved in tendering, especially small businesses.

Perhaps the most important lesson is not to get dragged into a bid that you don't think you can win. There is always euphoria when a company is able to attract their first major tender document; the salesperson thinks all their Christmases have come at once, having already won the bid in their imagination. But often you are just being wheeled in as a stalking-horse. Companies can go bankrupt gearing up for a big pitch which they have little chance of winning.

For the America's Cup, Keith spent several months researching whether the UK had a realistic chance of winning. Only when

Sir Keith Mills

Sir Keith Mills founded Air Miles International and was Chairman of Loyalty Management Group Ltd, the company which owns and manages the Nectar programme in the UK and licenses Air Miles programmes internationally.

Sir Keith was later International President and CEO of London 2012, the company that bid for and won the 2012 Olympic Games. Sir Keith is also a non-executive director of Tottenham Hotspur Plc and is Deputy Lieutenant of Kent. In 2007 Sir Keith announced his intention to lead Team Origin, which will compete for the next America's Cup Challenge.

he convinced himself this was the case did he put his energies into Team Origin.

With the Olympics, things were slightly different — this was a massive bid where resources were not an issue. But there are still powerful lessons that small business can learn from it.

First is the need to assemble a team behind the bid. What we saw on TV — Lord Coe or Tony Blair shaking hands with delegates — was only the tip of a giant iceberg. A huge team of hand-picked people worked behind the scenes to make the bid work.

The next is to be thorough. The team thought through every eventuality. They got to know all the International Olympic Committee delegates personally, and at the key meeting in Singapore, made sure they had a meeting with each one of them before the voting.

No stone was left unturned, and it was still

an incredibly close-run thing — most of the photographers were lined up in front of the Paris delegation as the result was due to be announced, and had to make an unseemly dash across to our team when it actually was.

And make sure that everyone is behind the bid. Just as important as pitching to the IOC was the day-to-day pitching to the local community in Stratford, to ensure that at least 80% wanted the Olympics. This was backed up by the appearance at Singapore of local young people, not just the usual fare of politicians, celebrities and seemingly endless rows of middle-aged chaps in blazers.

The lessons from the above? If you're responding to a tender, make sure your intelligence and preparation is top class, and also do significant internal selling to make sure everyone in your company is behind the bid (you'll need this support when times get tough during the delivery phase).

Sir Keith is clearly used to being a winner. He is also a non-executive director at Tottenham Hotspur. As a long-suffering supporter, this fact gives me a glimmer of hope. I'll give him the same Christmas list as I'm giving Santa: Champions League football every year, plus Ronaldo, Messi and Rooney. Please?

The Sky is Falling

Financial Times, 11th October 2008

When times are hard, it does seem that 'the sky is falling', as Chicken Licken famously said.

But, during recessions, obsessive entrepreneurs like me know it is an excellent time to do what comes naturally, to start and build a new business.

In a recession good people are more available and there are great deals to be had from suppliers. Once you are up and running, the best way to beat a recession is to sell your way out of it. If you could work out how to double your sales overnight, then the recession would be something that only affects your less nimble competitors.

A key to achieving this is to get everyone in your company, not just the salespeople, involved in sales. This is particularly important for outwardly undifferentiated service suppliers such as PR or marketing agencies and the more traditional professions like the law.

The websites of such businesses tend to show fascinating people with top-quality skills and experience. Which is great — but what is now required is for them to get out there, talking to customers.

And there's the rub; some are natural networkers, forever bringing in new clients, while for others, attending a networking event is second only to root canal work.

The solution is some simple training in the basic mechanics of sales, and maybe a bit of confidence-boosting. Sadly, training is often the first casualty as belts are tightened. This is of course a false economy; the most important assets for any business are your employees, the only people who will be able to get you out of a recession.

This will be a tough negotiation with your Finance Director, who will be sensibly reducing costs wherever they can, and 'discretionary spends' such as training are always prime candidates

this is how **yoodoo** it.

for the chop. But you need to explain that to retain your best staff you should invest in their skills, particularly in something that should get short-term results, such as good sales training.

One thing your people will learn on good sales training is the difference between 'hunters' and 'farmers': the former go after new business; the latter work with their existing client base, looking for new opportunities to sell. It is this latter role that most technical people in a business are best suited to, and are actually often very good at.

Farmers actually generate more sales than hunters: I've heard it said that for business service companies, 85% of their work comes from existing customers.

> Get everyone in your company, not just the salespeople, involved in sales

The ideal farmer has a streak of entrepreneurial opportunism in them. Clients are always happier to talk about their problems with a farmer than with a hunter, so your delivery people should always be on the lookout. This should not be just to sell existing services, but to be always asking what new products or services you might provide.

These may be close to what you already offer, and thus easily delivered. If the new request is for something radically different, then the farmer can offer to discuss the proposition with his or her bosses and see if it is feasible to deliver it profitably, on this one occasion, for this special client only.

This may be a one-off, but it could also be the start of a whole new business adventure, the opportunity to re-brand and re-position your company in a recession. Kentucky Fried Chicken did exactly that in 1991, during a recession, becoming 'KFC', and growing very quickly.

Perhaps that is what happened to Chicken Licken back in the recession of 1930; he cheered up and became 'Colonel Sanders'.

Everything is Negotiable

Financial Times, 28th February 2009

One of the major advantages of an economic downturn is that there are great deals to be had.

The challenge is that many of us are very bad at negotiating. For advice on this topic, I went to talk to Derek Arden.

Derek started his career in a bank in training and development, but soon found himself in major account management, negotiating with hard-nosed senior buyers at a large supermarket chain. He left the meetings with a strong feeling that he had come a distant second in the negotiation.

He resolved to read all the books available and go on courses to develop his negotiation skills. As a result, he became an expert on the subject, and has spent the last 8 years passing on this knowledge to all kinds of people.

He explains that where most of us fall down is in understanding the timing of a deal. This is aptly illustrated in his first major personal negotiating challenge, which was to arrange a favourable exit from the bank where he was working. Rather than force his own schedule on the bank's internal processes, he took his time, letting the bank dictate the schedule — as a result of which they were more generous with the terms.

> "Successful deal makers always ensure a win for both sides"

Derek believes strongly that the most important work on a deal is done in advance. The better prepared you are, the more likely you are to secure a good deal.

Another aspect is to see things from both sides. Successful deal makers always ensure a win for both sides, as they are always looking for a long-term relationship with the buyer. The hardest part of negotiation is always the price, especially if the buyer gives

this is how **yoodoo** it.

no clue about what they want to pay. Derek suggests always having three prices to hand.

First have a high 'dream' price. Buyers will accept more often than you might suspect, for example if they need your products or services in a hurry or are looking to empty a budget before the end of the financial year or risk losing it for the following year.

Then you should have a 'target' price, which represents what you feel the customer should pay, based on both value for money for them and a sensible profit for you.

Finally, you have a 'walk away' price, below which you cannot go, based on hard evidence from your delivery and finance people.

In a friendly negotiation you can even share this information, and a fair buyer should appreciate your openness and respond favourably. It is important to remember that very rarely do people buy the

Derek Arden

Derek Arden is an international negotiator, professional speaker and author. He is the strategic negotiation advisor to a number of companies and charities including Oxfam. He has run Masterclasses and spoken in 27 countries. He has recently featured on TV, radio and in the Financial Times.

www.derekarden.co.uk

cheapest offer; what is more important, especially in these hard times, is your providing proof of value for money.

Derek also trains people in advanced techniques including influencing and body language, but he says the basic principles remain simple. Prepare in advance, and ask good questions.

As Rudyard Kipling aptly put it, "I keep six honest serving-men; they taught me all I knew. Their names are What and Why and When, And How and Where and Who". These 'serving-men' are not the exclusive prerogative of a business elite. We can all use them to back up our sales efforts and turn them into deals where both sides emerge as winners.

Stars and Deal Makers

Financial Times, 26th January 2008

When I'm on holiday, street traders know immediately that I'll pay way over the odds for their souvenirs.

I leave car showrooms having paid list price. But I'm a salesman, aren't I? Yes, and I hope a very good one. But I am not a 'Deal Maker'.

To make sense of this apparent paradox, I went to see Dave Rogers, who honed his own deal-making skills as a banker in Japan and Hong Kong. Dave helped develop the Wealth Dynamics model, which includes a simple psychometric test for entrepreneurs.

In Wealth Dynamics, people are divided into eight different character types, or 'profiles'. One of these is 'Star', a person who is extrovert and intuitive. Great salespeople fall into this category, as do charismatic individuals with great personal brands, like George Foreman or Nigella Lawson. They attract potential opportunities but, if they are wise, hand over to someone else to do the actual deal, as they get bored by detail.

A successful Deal Maker is a people person with a great sense of timing

The ideal person to make the best of this opportunity has a 'Deal Maker' profile. Deal Makers are extrovert, like Stars, but 'grounded', which means that, unlike 'intuitive' Stars who tend to be driven by feelings (and to want things yesterday, as my friends keep telling me), they take a longer, more objective view, studying the world around them and making judgements based on what they learn.

Deal Makers are also great 'people people'. They have wide networks so they can identify the right individuals at the right time to make a deal work.

A good Deal Maker may strike a hard bargain, but the best ones are serially successful: people come back to them to do deals, which would not happen if they ripped people off.

Deal Makers have a natural eye for an opportunity. Examples include Rupert Murdoch and Donald Trump, who are on the lookout for deals in any business area; it does not just have to be in media or property.

Dave explained that Wealth Dynamics also has a model of how deals progress, using the metaphor of the seasons.

A deal begins with a 'spring' phase, where new and creative ideas bubble up and participants are full of optimism and enthusiasm. Then it moves to summer, when the energy is all about people and getting them around a table. What is vital at this stage is getting something down on paper that can go back and forth and form the basis of a negotiation.

Then the deal moves into autumn, when intellectual rigour is put into the process. This is when the lawyers and accountants should arrive; bringing them in too early can cause a deal to lose all its energy and grind to a halt. Finally, the deal moves into winter, when everything has been signed and sealed, and the deal is finally systematised. The initial promises are then turned into deliverables.

Above all, a successful Deal Maker is a people person with a great sense of timing. They leverage their network connections to get the right people involved at the right time so that the deal makes sense for everybody. And while a good Deal Maker may strike a hard bargain, the best ones ensure that the deal is always perceived as successful for both parties in the long term, so people will come back to them for the next opportunity.

The Wealth Dynamics model that Dave helped develop is based on Chinese philosophy, especially the I Ching (yijing), which is believed to have been around for over 3,000 years. Some things don't change.

Dave Rogers

Born in Canada of mixed Asian and European heritage, Dave Rogers is a skilled 'Deal Maker' and expert in entrepreneur coaching. He is author of two books, four audio & video programs and has appeared on radio, television and stage throughout the world.

Since 2001, Dave has conducted more than 100 entrepreneur coaching programmes to more than 2,500 entrepreneurs throughout Asia Pacific, Europe and North America and spoken to more than 25,000 delegates worldwide. Dave has coached multi-millionaires, bankers, top executives, medical professionals, internationally renowned artists, athletes, singers and dancers.

Dave is the Chief Coach with XL Results Foundation, the Immediate Past President of the Asia Professional Speakers Singapore, and the recipient of the Singapore Spirit of Enterprise Award for Entrepreneurship for 2007.

www.daverogers.net

Part Three:

Marketing and Communication

I've not always been hugely complimentary about marketing; sales people often aren't.

But I do understand the value added by marketing people, especially when they listen to what their salespeople are telling them about what real customers are saying and doing. So here are some pieces on this topic.

For the small business, especially in the service sector, you, the entrepreneur, are the brand. You can't get this across with conventional marketing tools like packaging or advertising. So how do you get out there and tell the world about yourself? In this section, I talk to experts on using Twitter and other 'social media', podcasts, and even writing a book, and also include a couple of pieces about my own particular 'route to attention' — professional speaking.

The section concludes with some more general pieces on marketing, PR and pricing.

A Wit and to Woo

Financial Times, 14th February 2009

Stephen Fry, as you all know, is an actor, presenter, author, director and unofficial national treasure.

What you probably also know is that he is also a mega-star on the social blogging site Twitter. Stephen is one of the most followed Twitterers in the world with over one million followers, and his following is growing daily.

I caught up with him at the Apple Store in Regent Street, where he was speaking as part of their 'Meet the Author' series. Despite his old-world appearance, he is a self-confessed gadget freak, having purchased the second Apple Macintosh in the UK (his friend and Hitchhiker's Guide author Douglas Adams bought the first).

Twitter is his latest enthusiasm. As one would expect from Stephen, this enthusiasm is driven by a sense of fun, but also based on sound reasoning.

Stephen is a natural for Twitter. He is his own man, and will speak his opinions loud and clear in the search for universal truth and beauty. He sets strict guidelines for how he uses the site, explaining that he only responds when inspired to do so, and apologises profusely that the large number of his followers means he cannot be everyone's friend, all the time.

He very occasionally uses Twitter to promote something that catches his fancy, such as a good cause, though he does make frequent references to projects he is working on. Generally he talks about whatever he feels passionate about, from endangered species to his favourite talking books. One time he got stuck in a lift for half an hour and posted some pictures, which made their way into several national newspapers. How's that for PR?

At his talk, he was asked if he thought the kids of today spent too much time on the internet. He observed that all through history, kids' elders and betters have been complaining similarly.

this is how **yoodoo** it.

Before the internet, it was about time wasted watching TV; before that, the radio was seen as a pointless distraction. In the 19th Century novelists like Jane Austen were regarded as facile and lacking in educational merit.

Asked what Oscar Wilde would have thought of Twitter, Stephen's guess was that Wilde would have been enchanted by the beauty and simplicity of the new system and would have been a keen Twitterer — but without any particular agenda, which is perhaps the secret of Stephen's success. By not selling, he sells himself very effectively.

> "Oscar Wilde would have been a keen Twitterer"

After the event, Stephen showed what a professional public figure he is. A queue of people, mostly in their 20s, formed to speak to him. He engaged each of them personally, signing long messages on books and scraps of paper, and happily having his photograph taken with them. Some gave him little notes, not with phone numbers but with their Twitter 'handles', hoping that Stephen would follow them.

I asked my own Twitter friends what benefits they received from the site. Alan Stevens, who provides media training and consultancy to CEOs, considers it the best recession-beating business tool he has come across, having received more business directly from Twitter in the last month than from all sources in the previous quarter.

Business author Ian Sanders uses Twitter for the promotion of his new book, Juggle! and secured a lucrative speaking engagement in Texas. Claire Richmond, who runs the site Find a TV Expert explains that if you work alone, the 'tweets' give you a sense of having people around you, like the buzz of an office.

For enthusiasts, Twitter means they can successfully build their on-line brands exactly as they choose, based on regular and direct interaction with followers and customers. So perhaps we are entering a new era of genuine celebrity, not based on cynicism massaged by Photoshop and public relations, but on curiosity and positive engagement with the world.

As one of Stephen's favourite poets, William Wordsworth, himself might have Twittered: "Bliss was it in that dawn to be alive, but to be young was very heaven!"

Stephen Fry

Stephen Fry is an actor, writer, comedian, author, television presenter and film director. He has appeared in A Bit of Fry and Laurie, Jeeves and Wooster, Wilde, the Blackadder series and is the host of the panel comedy trivia show, QI. He has recently presented his 2008 television series Stephen Fry in America and has chaired I'm Sorry I Haven't a Clue.
www.stephenfry.com

Network Management

Financial Times, Saturday 12th June 2009

Many of us feel guilty about our personal time management.

We think we should spend more of it reading, in the gym, or with our families. Now there is another new call on our precious time: to succeed in life and business, you must get involved in a host of on-line 'social media' networks.

There are many people who claim to have an unimaginable number of contacts via these media and can reel off impressive statistics for the tangible benefits they receive, implying that those who prefer to spend their time doing old-fashioned, proper work are inadequate and face extinction.

Some organisations even encourage their staff to spend a sensible amount of time on social media sites. But for most of us, it always comes back to the issue of allocating time. A small business owner has to balance the promised benefits against the real challenges of survival in a highly competitive marketplace.

This is the dilemma faced by Peter Roper. As well as working as a keynote speaker, facilitator and publisher, he is involved in two other businesses, which work together under the name Positive Ground. His daughter, Sara Beth, runs a successful company organising events for other speakers, and they also produce web-based radio shows.

Roper quickly realised that to promote his personal brand as a speaker he had to at least have his profile on all the major social media sites in case a potential customer happened to search for him.

This was a relatively simple process as he had a detailed speaker profile and a good set of photographs already prepared. He recommends an e-book to help you decide how much effort to put into each site: Social Media Marketing in 30 Minutes per Day by

Janet Helft neatly summarises which on-line networks are best for your business and how to use each of them to generate the right kinds of leads.

The best network sites also encourage you to select 'keywords'. As well as your own surname you can also specify specific subject areas of expertise or interest, in his case presentation skills for individuals and organisations. This makes life easy for the search engines and ensures that when you put 'Peter Roper' into Google, the first two results are from his own site, and the next two are the popular on-line networking sites Ecademy and LinkedIn.

Internet marketers will claim that if you get this on-line piece right, business will then flow in, as if by magic. While we all hope this is true, it is clearly wise to also go looking for new revenue in more conventional ways, too. However, it must be said that social media sites are ideal for promoting 'single-person brands'.

> "Social media sites are ideal for promoting single-person brands"

The other businesses in which Peter is involved have a slightly different challenge. They are organisations with brands, not people. However, they can use social media, too. They need to develop an 'online character'. Just like an individual, they need to be seen to have (and, behind this, to have) a wider intellectual and ethical purpose.

Both Peter and Sara Beth use social media, but they have differing styles. Between the two of them, they speak to a wide age range. Sara Beth feels more comfortable on Facebook, while Peter is used to the more complex, feature-driven Ecademy.

He is a more extrovert character, so looks for off-line opportunities such as networking events. She is happier to promote the business via e-mail and the internet. In both cases they use both business brands at different times for maximum benefit; for example Peter is active on micro-blogging site Twitter as himself, while Sara Beth is 'Positive Ground'.

this is how **yoodoo** it.

On-line networking, like entrepreneurship in general, is a team sport, and the clue to using these platforms most effectively is to realise that you should work with someone else who has complementary skills.

Underlying Peter and Sara Beth's online strategy is the understanding that they are primarily in the content business. Large numbers of network contacts in themselves do not benefit their business; you must also provide real value.

You cannot really have a proper, meaningful connection with several thousand people unless they are signed up to your newsletter, and you provide them not just sales messages, but relevant and useful content on a regular basis.

Peter Roper

Peter Roper is a keynote speaker, facilitator, best-selling author and publisher. He is also an expert in training people to present.

After a successful corporate career, Peter embarked on his own business in 1996, and has since presented to over 400,000 people on behalf of a wealth of businesses and organisations in many countries. He is a Fellow and Vice President of the PSA and is creator of Positive Ground Radio, a syndicated radio production company. www.peterroper.com

Social Media Marketing in 30 Minutes per Day by Janet Helft can be found at www.thirtyminutemarketing.com

The Podfather

Financial Times, 20th December 2008

Podcasting is a very hot topic for those who appreciate the importance of a serious web presence.

So I went to seek advice from one of the originators of the craft, Adam Curry, also known as 'The Podfather'.

His story is the classic combination of having talent and being in the right place at the right time. Being passionate about music, his first proper job was as a DJ on a pirate radio station before eventually going legitimate with MTV, providing chat and comment between the music videos.

The internet arrived in the early 90s and Adam decided it was fun and interesting long before there was even a World Wide Web. He made the crucial observation that all the cool kids who watched him on MTV were also on-line and wanted to communicate with him directly.

He personally registered the domain name www.mtv.com and then set about finding ways to make money from this new audience. Adam realised that what they wanted to do was relatively simple: browse content, archive information, chat to each other and send e-mails.

Advertisers then came knocking on his door and he built up a very successful new media agency showing traditional companies such as Proctor and Gamble, Budweiser and Reebok how to leverage their brands on the Web.

Eventually, he decided to sell his company, a decision seen as very foolish at the time; Adam remembers appearing on the cover of a well-known business magazine with a dunce's cap Photoshopped onto his head. A few months later the dot-com crash turned him from idiot to visionary.

After the traditional period having fun, flying helicopters and buying a castle in Europe, he became re-engaged with technology, this time spotting the potential of the cool new device from Apple, the iPod. While others just saw music on the move, he saw an opportunity for his audience to subscribe to audio content and download talk shows. Podcasting, broadcasting not to the airwaves but to an iPod, was born.

There is no inherent magic about pod-casting; all it does is provide on-line audio, connecting people who cannot get exposure on traditional channels with listeners who want bite-sized chunks of content when it suits them, not necessarily at a particular broadcast time. Adam's view is that while on-line

"Any business can turn its successful customer stories into podcasts for relatively little expense"

video should be no longer than three minutes long (I blame the MTV generation), on-line audio works well at around 25 minutes.

He called his show The Daily Source Code as a nod to his early audience of software geeks, and now has over 500,000 subscribers. The listeners themselves provide much of the content; he has a coterie of people who he considers to have 'savant' status, with experience in specialist areas. One is 'Atomic Rod', who may or may not be on a nuclear submarine somewhere, but who can provide arcane information, such that atomic waste is not, as you might imagine, 45 gallon drums oozing green liquid, but comes in small blue blocks, rather like those items you find in toilet bowls.

Making money out of your podcast is simple once you have a large number of regular listeners. Businesses will want to 'sponsor' you by sticking an advertorial piece on the end of your podcast. Clearly you need to be convinced that this will add value to your offer rather than detract from it; otherwise it is a short-term gain only. A good sponsor will understand that a hard sell will turn people off, but that to be seen as providing accurate and clear information is a 'win' for them.

Any business can turn its successful customer stories into podcasts for relatively little expense compared to a traditional advertising campaign. This will give your happy customers a chance to tell the world your success stories for you, and as they do this, increase their loyalty to you.

The MTV generation now has significant spending power. It makes very good sense to send them interesting content and this week's special offer directly to their cool white headphones.

Adam Curry

Adam Curry was born in the United States and spent most of his childhood in Amsterdam. He began his broadcasting career in The Netherlands as a teenager, and then returned to the US to become one of MTV's on-air personalities in 1987. He was the host of the 1980s' Top 20 Countdown on MTV, and internet users know him as one of the first celebrities to emerge on the World Wide Web.

During his tenure at MTV (1987-94) he also hosted a New York City radio show and a nationally syndicated radio programme called Hitline USA. Since the early 1990s Curry has been involved in Web technology and media, first as the founder of a design and hosting company, then as an executive with a marketing and communication agency and now as a high-profile personality in the development of podcasting.

http://dailysourcecode.com

The Business of Speaking

Financial Times, 19th July 2008

Most of my working life is spent on the speaking circuit, which means I often share the stage with other speakers.

Some are professionals like me; others clearly have the gift and could make a living as a speaker if they set their mind to it. Most are less natural speakers but often are looking for some top tips for a particular event where they have been asked to 'say a few words'.

To deal with the last challenge first. A good talk is a planned talk. Not word-for-word, but the overall structure.

Start with the end, and your call to action or great closing comment. Then think about the beginning, with a good opening, explaining why you have been invited to speak to them and what you are going to cover in your talk.

In the middle, tell stories, which all have a beginning (a problem), a middle (what happened), and an end (the outcome and associated learning points). Over the years I have built up a huge library of good stories, both from my own experience and from the wide range of business people I have interviewed for this column.

It is also important to understand that an audience is motivated in three different ways. Some are 'auditory' and like to listen, so the words are very important. Others are 'visual' and like to see images, so do make sure your presentation includes pictures and even video, not just diagrams and bullet points. The third and most important driver is 'kinaesthetic', which is all about appealing to the audience's emotions.

The usual technique is to tell a story and then explain how you felt at the time; if you have developed some empathy with the audience, they will feel that emotion as well.

If this talk went well, you should consider speaking more often. It is a great way to promote your business. If you do, then you should definitely join the Professional Speaking Association, the PSA. There are regular local chapter meetings, as well as an annual conference.

At these events, you will find other professional speakers, including Fellows of the Association such as myself, willing to share their secrets on every aspect of the business, from platform skills to making money on the internet.

Pitch your talk to your friends first. If you have built up a good network of corporate chums who find you interesting and amusing, then try to sell to them. If they won't book you for their conference, then it is unlikely anyone else will.

If you speak regularly, always ask for money. The first fee is the hardest and it never gets completely painless, so it is a very good idea to get an experienced salesperson or even your spouse or partner to do the negotiating on your behalf.

> "Speak at every possible opportunity"

Speak at every possible opportunity: Rotary, Round Table, Women's Institutes, local fêtes, anywhere that will let you practice the craft. For that is what it is, something that you can work on for the rest of your life, if you get the speaking bug.

You may even end up as a full-time, professional speaker — if you do, welcome aboard! You will find yourself pitched into strange surroundings, sometimes with an incorrect brief, a poor sound system and a hostile audience; it can and will go horribly wrong, now and then. When it does, you need the skills and self-belief to pick yourself up, dust yourself off, and start all over again at tomorrow's event.

But even if you don't end up as a professional, you can still present in a professional manner, and both give pleasure to people and promote your business — a very pleasant 'win/win'.

The Professional Speaking Association:
www.professionalspeakersassociation.co.uk

this is how **yoodoo** it.

In Your Own Write

Financial Times, 1st December 2007

I'm often asked "Mike, how do I write a best-selling business book?"

My reply is always the same: "Get a professional to help you." I then direct them to my good friend Mindy Gibbins-Klein, known as 'The Book Midwife'.

'Midwife' is a good metaphor, as writing a book might well involve 9 months' labour and considerable pain. Sadly, there are no drugs to ease this pain — or to give you extra inspiration: what worked for Coleridge and Hunter S Thompson probably won't work for a business book.

The first step is to think through why you're doing this in the first place. Unless you're famous, you must be sure you have something fresh to say and have a clear idea of who you want to say it to.

Mindy helps aspiring writers think these issues through. Then there is the actual business of planning the book. She does not believe in the concept of 'writer's block', which she says is a result of inadequate preparation. If you have really prepared your book the words will flow and they will often be pretty good words.

Many people write better than they think they can, she believes. With a lot of planning before they write and a modicum of editing afterwards, they can produce a worthwhile book.

The actual business of publishing has been revolutionised by technology. It is now cheap and easy to self-publish, and, more importantly, cheap and easy to self-publish well, producing a book that looks and feels professional.

I asked her about the value added by a name brand (our Beermat guides, for example, are published by Random House). Mindy is open-minded about this — the brand does add cachet, but it's hard to get publishing deals out of these people and the terms are usually not good. And do people care that much about publishing brands, anyway? Hands up all those who know the publisher of The Da Vinci Code... The author is the brand.

Even if you have a major publisher, you still have to promote the book yourself. Big publishers turn out many books a year, and with the best will in the world cannot devote vast resources to publicising an individual book, unless they believe it will be a massive bestseller like the Harry Potter series.

Clearly if you are a speaker you have a big advantage here. You can sell your self-published book from the 'back of the room'. If you do not have an audience to hand, the task is harder but not impossible. Sell it online. Have promotional postcards made and hand them out — Mindy cites an author who sold 6,000 books this way, which is more than most professionally published business books sell.

> "Have something fresh to say and a clear idea of who you want to say it to"

You should always get some 'name' endorsements to go on the jacket. I don't mean Z-listers from Big Brother; I mean people who are respected in your area of expertise. This is a very good test of your networking ability, calling in favours from the great and the good, to add credibility to your masterpiece. This is not as difficult as it seems; most people, assuming they like you in the first place, will be flattered to have their name on the cover of your book.

But here's a top tip: write a wide selection of possible reviews yourself and send them to the VIPs, so they can choose one. This takes away the time and effort in composing something witty and original for a book they are actually unlikely to spend a lot of time reading. Even if your book does not become a bestseller (or even a 'business bestseller', which is a much more humble aspiration), it is a fantastic brochure for you and your expertise.

If it does take off, it will turn out to be the best publicity your business ever had. I'm certainly very optimistic. As you may have already worked out, this book itself was developed and delivered under her expert guidance.

Mindy Gibbins-Klein

Mindy Gibbins-Klein is best known as The Book Midwife and is co-founder of Ecademy Press business publishing. She is an international speaker, writing and publishing strategist and a leading book coach who has helped over 300 experts write and publish their books; many of them gaining bestseller status and significant media attention.

www.bookmidwife.com

Marketing on a Beermat

Financial Times, 9th August 2008

There are many characteristics that are common
to most successful entrepreneurs, including vision,
confidence, ambition and drive.

But a common feature of all the ones I know and like is that they
care passionately about the people who use their product or
service: their customers. This, I discover from Chris West's new
book, Marketing on a Beermat, is the 'marketing mindset'. And I
thought it was the prerogative of sales!

Chris's book is not about the kind of marketing you would find at
a large organisation, with endless research, obsession with brand
values and a fortune spent on advertising. It's about marketing
for start-ups, where the competitive landscape is only partially
understood, budgets are small or non-existent, and decisions are
based more on gut instinct than exhaustive research.

To write the book, Chris drew on his own experiences in
marketing and PR, but also took advice from experts such as
Louse Third, author of PR on a Beermat, internet marketer Peter
Bennett, and Graham Michelli, who started his own marketing
agency after spells at ICI and Kawasaki.

Small businesses have to rely on relentless street-level activity,
encouraging word of mouth referrals and gaining free PR wherever
possible. Proper branding will come later; for now, more important
is the personal brand of the entrepreneur themselves, and how
convincing they are that people should buy from them rather than
another supplier.

Advertising is one area where small businesses can get things
horribly wrong. Led on by 'brand-building' ads on TV, they waste
money 'promoting the brand'. This is what Graham Michelli calls
'coo-ee advertising'. If you are a car company, you can afford
to do this (or could, before the recession, anyway). If you are a

start-up, you cannot. Ads must contain a specific call to action from the target.

Instead, try getting free publicity... it can be done, and the book shows how. There are many publications, on- and off-line, desperate for copy, but what they are looking for is stories, not just a list of product features.

Alongside the essentially intuitive 'marketing mindset', the key to good marketing is to have a clear, reasoned understanding of who you are and where you fit into the market. All businesses should ask themselves Chris's 'Five Questions':

What pain do we solve? This usually relates to money, time or effort.

Who for? You must have a target market. Entrepreneurs often think their product is 'for everybody', but nothing is for everybody.

> "Have a clear, reasoned understanding of who you are and where you fit into the market"

Where, among people you can reach and who have money to pay for your offer, is the pain most acutely felt?

What are we going to do about it? This has to be expressed in terms of products, which Chris defines as 'clearly specified and priced bundles of benefits, which can be sold repeatedly and profitably'.

Give one good reason why people should switch to you: that old marketing regular, the 'USP' (Unique Selling Point).

And finally, 'Says who?' — establish your credibility.

These questions form the basis of your strategy — a word that Chris says is often assumed only to refer to huge corporates (and to imply Harvard Doctorates before you understand it), but is actually common sense and highly applicable to businesses of all sizes.

Marketing may not be as arcane as some of its proponents like to claim, but it is many-faceted. To illustrate this, Chris presents a 'cast list' of model businesses, taking them all through the issues he discusses, to ensure that the book presents the right kind of marketing for a range of enterprises, from a self-employed consultant to a high-tech start-up with global ambitions.

The book, which is admirably succinct despite covering a lot of ground, ends with 'The Ten Commandments of Marketing'. They are all solid gold, but for me, the final one is the most important: 'your most valuable resource is the goodwill of your existing customers'. If you communicate your benefits clearly and treat your customers well, they will do much of your marketing for you, by far the best option.

Chris West

Chris West is a professional writer. He has written fiction, including a quartet of crime novels set in modern China, and travel, but is best known for his work on entrepreneurship. He is co-author of The Beermat Entrepreneur. He is also an experienced marketer and author of Marketing on a Beermat. Chris can be contacted at: **www.chriswest.info**

Graham Michelli

Graham Michelli's career has focused on new business and new brand development both as a consultant to a wide variety of companies, from tiny to huge, and as a serial entrepreneur in his own right. He is a Fellow of the Chartered Institute of Marketing and Liveryman of the Worshipful Company of Marketors.

Marketing on a Beermat is published by Random House Business Books

The Price is Right

Financial Times, 6th February 2008

Sales down? Margins squeezed? Worried about
the recession?

If so, here is a top tip: put your prices up!

I often run regular sales workshops with early stage companies
and invariably find that they are not charging enough for their
products or services. They feel that in a competitive market they
should be forever shaving their margins and lowering their prices.

The reality is that if you are perceived as cheap, people will
worry about buying from you. Most people prefer paying a proper
price so long as they feel that they are getting good quality and
value for money. These are the customers you should be targeting,
not the ones who seem to be forever complaining about your prices.

This is particularly true with service businesses, but it also
applies to products, or at least
products of any complexity, where
quality is an issue. The only place
where you are really forced
into a price war is 'commodity'
products, where what you make is
indistinguishable from that of your
rivals — petrol, for example.

> "Most people prefer paying a proper price so long as they feel that they are getting good quality and value for money"

Most products have a service
element attached to them.
Customers want them delivered on time. They also want to receive
prompt, friendly and effective service when there is a problem.
These elements cost money, and should always be factored into
your price, which then has to be explained to the customer.

Software is a good example of a mixture of both product and
service. It may look like a product, all nicely packaged in a box,
but usually requires support, which can be very expensive.

Sadly, many software companies don't understand this and price their products far too low, essentially by looking at the cost of production, rather than at the costs of development or, more relevant still, measuring the benefits the customers will eventually receive.

A good example of how to get pricing right is Broadbean, a company run by Dan McGuire. He had worked for a couple of years in the recruitment industry and saw a gap in the market with the arrival of internet job-finding sites such as Monster.com.

Recruitment agencies began to put their vacancies on these sites but the process was time-consuming and tedious. Dan's plan was to automate the process of posting job vacancies using a clever piece of software.

He suspected that the recruitment industry was tight on margins, so he priced his software very low, starting at around £100 a month. He spent a long time in the doldrums, not even taking a salary; not only were recruitment agencies loathe to spend even £100, he also had a number of competitors, all offering what appeared to be a similar service (though they were, in fact, inferior) for £10 a month less. He knew a price war would bankrupt his company, so he took a radical step. He tripled the price of his software.

This had an immediate effect; potential customers were initially very sceptical, but at least he had started a dialogue with them, discussing how he could possibly justify charging so much.

Dan believed in his product and could show that not only did his software save considerable manual labour for the agencies; it also quickly paid for itself many times over, thus providing excellent value for money.

Customers soon understood this, and became prepared to pay for it.

It is much easier to find ways of improving your products or services than it is to reduce your costs. Look at the occasions when your existing customers were particularly satisfied and did not quibble about your costs. Invariably, it was because you provided excellent service. All you need to do is to provide these elements and more to all your customers, all of the time.

If you do, they will usually pay a sensible price. Usually. But sometimes you find yourself dealing with an experienced negotiator, such as a purchasing director, who is very effective at asking for discounts.

The message here is 'Don't panic!' I recently moderated a conference for purchasing directors, and they all said the same thing: it is never just about price; what they are really looking for is value for money. If you can honestly justify your price on the basis of good quality, delivery and customer service, they are prepared to listen.

The idea for putting his price up certainly worked for Dan McGuire. He now has over 40 staff and was recently awarded 'Young Entrepreneur of the Year' by Real Business magazine. He has plans to open up on the West Coast of America and in the Far East so he can provide 24/7 coverage for his international customers. This coverage is a very valuable extra benefit, which I am sure will be reassuringly expensive.

Dave McGuire

Dan McGuire is widely regarded as one of the UK's top young entrepreneurs, with a string of prestigious awards to his name. His first company, Broadbean Technology, was sold to DMGT in October 2008 and he is the founder of social enterprise The Two Hour Initiative which brings entrepreneurs together to promote business in schools.

Have You Got News For Them?

Financial Times, 1st March 2008

There are many upsides to being a columnist for
the FT, but one downside: I receive too many press
releases from PR agencies.

It's not that the callers aren't nice. They're delightful: people
in PR companies seem to have First Class Honours Degrees from
the University of Cheerfulness. But they don't have a story that is
right for me. I discussed this problem with Louise Third of Integra
Communications, who has written the eBook PR on a Beermat.

Louise is a great believer in the power of PR, and that you can
exercise this power yourself, without an agency, if you set about it
the right way. She runs an excellent do-your-own-PR course at the
British Library, called 'Have You Got News For Us?', with her friend
Maisha Frost, a business journalist on the Daily Express.

"Most journalists
don't actually mind
being called up by
entrepreneurs with
good stories"

Her first tip is to work out exactly
what your actual story is. The fact
that you are an interesting company
with many products is not enough;
what excites editors are real-life
stories of customers with problems,
how you solved them, and the happy
consequences. This is exactly how all
your customer case studies and press
releases should be structured: in the style of a novel, with a
beginning, a middle and an end.

The story must also resonate with the reader, so think carefully
which publication you are targeting, and why their readers might
be interested in the first place. Most press releases naturally
gravitate towards the national newspapers with their large
circulations, but it is usually more effective to target specialist
magazines in the particular market where you operate.

Good examples are the guest publications lampooned on Have I Got News For You, such as Arthritis News, Polyester Digest and Winking World (I only made one of those up) — but read and enjoyed by their target audiences.

Trade journals are always hungry for copy, and will even provide names of freelance journalists who can advise on exactly which types of stories the publications are looking for.

Be careful about publications who offer 'advertorial', where buying a full-page of advertising will guarantee a favourable write-up; your potential customers and buyers can often see through this pretence.

The most surprising feedback from Louise was that most journalists don't actually mind being called up by entrepreneurs with good stories; they actually prefer to speak directly to the originator wherever possible.

Louise Third

Louise Third, Director of Integra Communications Limited, and author of PR on a Beermat, is a highly experienced and versatile entrepreneur. Her interest in small firms and enterprise has taken her though a career as a business adviser, consultant, media spokesperson and director of her own public relations company.

www.integracommunications.co.uk

Maisha Frost

National media reporter Maisha Frost has covered the UK enterprise and the SME sector for more than a decade. Her particular interests include manufacturing, green and community businesses, technology and innovative financing.

But she advises that you do your homework first, not only in the relevance of the story, but also in the timing of your call. Journalists work to very specific copy deadlines, and you should definitely avoid calling them just when they are in the process of 'putting their column to bed'.

Louise's final tip is that 'a picture tells a thousand words'. You should provide good quality photographs of the principals involved in the story, especially if there is a local angle. When I speak at public events I am inevitably asked for any local connection and then photographed outside the venue with some local dignitary: this hopefully represents brand enhancement for both of us.

Another press release has just arrived, about some corporate statistics in which I have no interest. If you work for a big PR company, please think of someone really interesting for me to interview. Perhaps you could find me a government minister who can explain exactly how they are genuinely reducing red tape for small businesses, or making the process of claiming business expenses as fun and interesting as it is for MPs. Now that would be a good story!

Part Four:

Finance

More than any other aspect of business, finance can create terror in otherwise sane, sensible people.

It may come from school, where some people decided they were 'rubbish' at maths. It may come from hearing bankers talk about the complexities of derivatives. Or it may come from the belief that if you mess up your finances, you can end up in jail.

In fact, basic financial common sense for the small business is just that, basic common sense. Add to it a little knowledge — or someone on the team with a lot of knowledge (your Finance Cornerstone if you are building a business, the right outsourced bookkeeper if you are smaller), and you're sorted. There is no need to fear this topic at all.

A more reasonable reaction to finance is just boredom. The wise entrepreneur overcomes this, too. And certainly, the finance people I spoke to did not fit into the boring-man-in-a-suit stereotype at all. As you will see...

Your Local Bookkeeper

Financial Times, 5th September 2009

Most sole traders aren't going to go on to build great companies, but they still create value for themselves, their customers and society.

And they are arguably just as intrepid as more ambitious entrepreneurs: by deciding to work alone, they commit themselves to having to master all aspects of business, while the company-builder can go out and seek cornerstones (virtual ones at first, of course).

But, of course, that's where the finance bogeyman jumps out at them. By finance, of course, I don't mean the kind of stuff that goes on in the Square Mile and on Wall Street, but the 'money side of business'.

Many sole traders suffer from a pathological fear of the common spreadsheet, as can be seen if you visit their offices and notice the file of unpaid invoices next to a plastic bag full of unsorted receipts. But they can't afford, and don't really need, a virtual Finance Director. What's the way out of this problem?

I was delighted to meet Alex King from The Local Bookkeeper, which as Ronseal's advertising slogan aptly puts it, 'does exactly what it says on the tin'.

Their concept is simple: to let small businesses get on with what they do best, which is serving their customers, supported by someone who can explain in plain and simple English what is really going on financially so they can make the right decisions. The Local Bookkeeper has over 30 offices across the country, run by chartered accountants and qualified bookkeepers, which provide bookkeeping, payroll, management accounts and credit control services.

The company is actually a spin-off from a larger one, Franaccounts, which specialises in delivering accounting services for franchises and national businesses.

Example Local Bookkeeper customers include taxi drivers, who have no interest in finance as such — apart from when they had that Nick Leeson in the back of their cab, once — but just require the minimum amount of work in order to prepare their accounts.

Alex is keen to point out that The Local Bookkeeper also works with more ambitious businesses that seek to outsource these basic but essential functions. What all of their customers share is a desire to provide great services or products and a secret dread of evenings spent trying to manage their accounts.

People become entrepreneurs for a number of reasons: to make money, to control their own destiny, to make a difference to their own and their family's lives; essentially to have more fun. VAT returns and management accounts don't qualify as fun for most people.

But strange as it may seem to those of us who loathe spreadsheets, fun for The Local Bookkeeper is all about getting your accounts in order and then providing pro-active advice on how best to scale your business without you going broke in the process.

> "Many sole traders suffer from a pathological fear of the common spreadsheet"

This should enable sole traders and start-up entrepreneurs to enjoy life more by allowing them to spend more time with their customers and their families, not poring over spreadsheets deep into the night.

Alex King

Alex King previously held the position of Group Marketing Director at Franaccounts, the UK's leading British Franchise Association affiliated accountancy firm. He is a member of the Chartered Institute of Marketing (CIM) and Market Research Society as well as acting on the Committee for CIM Sussex.

The Local Bookkeeper can be found at: **www.thelocalbookkeeper.co.uk**

The Finance Cornerstone

Financial Times, 23rd August 2008

One of the symptoms of a credit crunch moving seamlessly into a recession is the unfortunate chore of the entrepreneur having to spend more time with their bank manager.

This might be to obtain more credit to cope with a short-term cash-flow problem, or to explain the restructuring required to take best advantage of unpredictable market conditions. Whatever the desired outcome, this is unlikely to be a meeting which either party regards with keen anticipation.

The problem is that the entrepreneur and the bank manager speak two completely different languages. The entrepreneur likes to talk about new ideas and opportunities, about changing the world and making a difference and being recognised in the street. The bank manager is probably under strict instructions from above to reduce the risk in their portfolio, and can only express this in the language of the spreadsheet and the bottom line.

"Don't force entrepreneurs to understand finance: you might as well try and teach fish to knit pullovers"

Many years ago in my first start-up our CEO went to open a bank account. He was back very quickly and in a bad mood, so we realised the meeting had not gone well. In his view, the bank manager was an idiot; he had not understood how clever our CEO was, how we clearly had an unbeatable business proposition and how much money we all were all going to make, including the bank.

Our CEO was ultimately right about this. We did indeed sell the company for a lot of money only 5 years later. But back on day one we had a small problem; we did not even have a bank account.

The solution to this problem? Don't force entrepreneurs to understand finance: you might as well try and teach fish to knit

this is how **yoodoo** it.

pullovers. Instead, the entrepreneur should take on, and listen to, a Finance Cornerstone.

This is very unlikely to be a full-time employee from day one; most people have a 'virtual' Finance Cornerstone, someone who comes perhaps one day a month and puts some order to your receipts and invoices in preparation for submitting your accounts.

There is an important distinction between an accountant and a Finance Cornerstone. An accountant is essentially reactive; they will do your books and then tell you what has happened. "Sorry, you've gone broke. Here's why." A Finance Cornerstone is pro-active; they tell you in advance that unless you do certain things, you will go broke at some time in the future.

Even if they only come in one day a month, they understand your business and can advise on how to scale up when times are good, and how to scale down when they are not.

As they speak the language of the bank manager, they should always accompany you to any such meetings. The entrepreneur should make some introductory remarks, and then leave the running of the meeting to the Finance Cornerstone.

In particular, any promises made about the provision of security or repayment of loans should be made by someone who not only understands the mindset of the bank manager, but who is also more likely to be trusted to keep those promises. And if circumstances change and repayment terms need to be negotiated, this is best done by a professional, who will present a case that is based on facts rather than emotions.

In my first start-up we were lucky that another of our shareholders, the CEO's brother, was a vice-president of Goldman Sachs, and thus able to smooth things over with the bank.

If you are not in this happy situation, then I recommend one of the organisations that provide virtual Finance Cornerstones, such as fd unlimited www.fdunlimited.com.

They provide part-time and interim finance directors, and well as a recruitment service. fd unlimited's founder and CEO David

Bloom told me a typical story about one of their clients, an owner-manager who had been in business for over ten years, but had become exhausted.

Five years previously, he had half the number of staff but double the pre-tax profits, but could not work out why. A member of David's team looked at the problem, examined the margins, and came up with a list of customers.

The client looked at this list with some affection, until he was shown that these were the customers that were actually losing him money. He went back to them all with a more sensible pricing strategy; some understood the problem, and accepted the price rise, others left in a huff.

The following year, turnover was down by about 15%, but profits were up 60%. All that had happened in the previous five years was that the owner manager had become pre-occupied with running the business, and had lost sight of the financial basics, which had made him strong in the past.

fd unlimited addresses these and many other relatively straightforward financial challenges for overstressed entrepreneurs. They are just the type of people to have by your side, especially when it is time to visit your bank manager.

David Bloom

David Bloom is CEO of fd unlimited, who provide part-time, interim and full-time finance directors, financial controllers, finance Managers, board advisors and back-office services.

Fund from Revenue!

Financial Times, 14th June 2008

One of the most common questions in my inbox is "how do I get funding for my new business?"

Of course it all depends on exactly what type of business you are running and where you are located. In certain parts of the UK there are considerable government grants or interest-free loans available. And there are always 'business angels' (more on these later!). However, my view is that by far the best way to fund a business is through revenue.

Any service-based business should be able to do this; if you find a problem and solve it, then someone will pay you, ideally with money up front.

If you cannot negotiate such advantageous terms, look for a bank manager who is impressed by your business idea, your team and — this is the key — your already burgeoning order book. You should then be able to fund your business through a bank loan without putting your house on the line.

For companies with physical products rather than services, it's not as easy. Product development typically requires investment in machinery, stock and other expensive items, and this usually involves external investment and the entrepreneur losing much of their precious equity in the process.

But even with product companies, smart deal-making can get around the funding problem. A great example of how to do it was demonstrated by Harold Goddijn and the satellite navigation company TomTom,

Bill Clinton very kindly opened up the ultra-secret US satellite system, allowing anyone to find out where they were via GPS (Global Positioning System). This created a buzz around 'location-based services', supposedly the next 'killer application' for personal organisers and mobile phones.

Once you knew where you were, you could potentially use these devices to find a great deal in a local restaurant, network with any chums nearby or access a constantly updated guide to the area.

Sadly, most of the early applications of location-based services turned out to be ahead of their time, but Harold and his team had a vision of a reasonably priced, easy-to-use consumer device in your vehicle, which would get you where you wanted to go.

TomTom's success depended on striking two important deals. First, they needed a set of content-rich digital maps, so began negotiations with the small number of people who owned these very complex and expensive pieces of intellectual property. A deal was struck with Tele Atlas, involving a mutually beneficial revenue model based on the promise of large numbers of units that would be shipped if the price per map was kept reasonable.

> "Even with product companies, smart deal-making can get around the funding problem"

The second deal was between TomTom and their retailers. Many industries, particularly in the IT world, have a complex set of channels including master distributors, value-added resellers, standard distributors and dealers.

This means that a product might be handed down this chain through several pairs of hands, each of which takes a margin. This erodes profit, can confuse end-users and often leads to 'channel conflicts' where different people in the chain are fighting over the same piece of business.

TomTom decided to strike deals directly with retailers like PC World and Halfords, cutting out the intermediaries and making sure that margins remained viable and that the consumer could buy a reasonably-priced product.

These deals meant they were able to grow their company through revenue, and just before they floated on the stock market in Amsterdam in 2005 they still owned 100% of the equity.

Harold and his team have used the floatation money wisely, making strategic acquisitions and growing the company to over 1,600 people. They have consistently refined their business model, keeping in-house core activities such as hardware and software development while outsourcing hardware manufacture, manufacturing logistics and distribution.

Satellite navigation is an apt metaphor for any business, even if it is not as successful or high- tech as TomTom. Business is essentially simple; it is just about knowing where you are and where you want to get to. And if you do smart deals, you may not even have to borrow the money to get there.

Harold Goddijn

Harold Goddijn studied Economics at Amsterdam University and started his career with a venture capital firm. He then founded Psion Netherlands BV in 1989, as a joint venture with Psion Plc, and in 1991 co-founded TomTom with Peter-Frans Pauwels and Pieter Geelen.

He continued to lead Psion Netherlands BV, developing it into a key European distributor for Psion. In 1998, he was appointed Managing Director of Psion Computers and served on the Board of Psion Plc from 1998 to 1999.

Harold was appointed Chief Executive Officer of TomTom in 2001.

www.tomtom.com

'Where's The Pain?'

Financial Times, 10th May 2008

In our Beermat model, when you want to start a business, you go down to a pub, and ask "Where's the pain?"

The more intense the pain out there, then the more likely people are going to want to pay money to have it taken away. If your idea involves a service, you can quickly build a lifestyle or boutique business, financing the entire enterprise on revenue plus, possibly, a small amount of bank debt.

If you are looking to develop a physical product or more far-reaching service, you will probably require some investment. You will then discover another 'pain': yours; the excruciating experience of raising money.

> "Is the business in a hot area, and how good is the team?"

My first tip for anyone raising money is never to attempt this with anyone much younger than you. The bright young spark in front of you may have several business school degrees and a spell at McKinsey and Company under their belt, but they have no experience of starting or building a business.

Some are just too 'clever' to have any understanding of your passion for what you are trying to do. Others relish picking holes in your argument and then dismiss you with the sort of sneering arrogance that explains why their parents sent them away to boarding school in the first place.

As an antidote to these ghastly people, I went and had a chat to Simon Clark of Fidelity Ventures, a business funder who actually understands the realities of growing businesses.

After sorting out Reuters' pre-internet business he built Reuters.com and worked with Reuters Ventures, investing in start-up companies. He later used his finance skills to take public TheStreet.com, an on-line stock broking service. A public floatation is even more painful than raising private equity, so he took a break and then moved to Fidelity Ventures.

Fidelity Ventures typically invest between £5m and £15m, focusing on hi-tech companies, using their experience both as massive users of technology as well as investors in software, consumer systems and communications companies such as Seatwave, Curam, Asset Control and Colt.

I asked Simon what he looked for in a new investment, and he said that the two big questions are: "is the business in a hot area?" and "how good is the team?"

He also said that he, and other capital providers, particularly like working with CEOs with whom they have worked before, whom they know, like and trust. So my best advice for any high technology start-up is to spend as much of your first 'friends and family' money as you can on an experienced CEO with excellent contacts in the investment community.

Simon says that much of his time is spent developing relationships with likely CEOs for businesses he funds. At the other end of the process, he also spends time building contacts with those large organisations that might be interested in acquiring those businesses later. He has quarterly meetings with Cisco, who have a track record in buying the best start-ups.

Simon still has a yearning for the good old days of 1995, when a company like Reuters Ventures could easily invest in new companies which didn't tick the standard financial boxes but looked in some almost indefinable way 'quite interesting': even if the investment failed, they would have learnt a lot from the experience.

One such investment was actually named after someone who was a 'pain', or rather, as the Dictionary defines it, 'uncultured, ignorant or stupid, of lower intelligence than you yourself': a Yahoo.

The word 'Yahoo' also has another definition, of course: the cry of triumph you might make when your relatively modest investment turns into serious money.

Simon Clark

Simon Clark focuses on investment opportunities in emerging European and Israeli technology companies for Fidelity Ventures. He is currently on the Board of Directors of a number of hi- tech start-ups.

Prior to joining Fidelity in 1999, Simon was Chief Financial Officer and General Manager, International, of TheStreet.com, a leading financial news website. In this role he managed two rounds of venture fundraising, a strategic investment and the IPO.

He spent 7 years at Reuters in various finance, IT and general management positions and, in 1995, established and ran Reuters.com. He qualified as a Chartered Accountant at Price Waterhouse.

Simon represents Fidelity as a committee member for the British Private Equity and Venture Capital Association (BVCA), the representative body for the UK private equity and venture capital industry.

www.fidelityventures.com

this is how **yoodoo** it.

I Believe in Angels

Financial Times, 15th March 2008

Have you ever wondered what makes very rich people happy?

We get a rather skewed view from the populist press, who enjoy telling tales of conspicuous consumption and bad behaviour. My personal experience is that most wealthy people seem to spend a significant part of their time worrying about how to prevent their children turning into this stereotype, whilst simultaneously wanting to give something back to the world that has treated them so well.

I was discussing this topic with David Giampaolo, who is a successful entrepreneur turned investor and mentor — a way of life that he finds intensely enjoyable.

David's entrepreneurial career began mowing lawns in Florida. He then set up a small gym — which grew into a large one, and ultimately into Fitness Holdings Europe, which he sold in 1999 during a stock-market boom (remember them?).

Next, he joined Pi Capital, a group of like-minded people all looking to invest in up-and-coming companies. Pi Capital is now a group of 300 people, an interesting combination of self-made millionaires and top FTSE executives, who meet on a regular basis to hear presentations from the great and the good on a wide variety of subjects.

> "This is exactly the kind of 'angel' investor an entrepreneur needs; someone who will take an active interest in the business"

Philanthropy is a common topic, but another focus of the meetings is what might or might not make a good potential investment for the members, who opt in on a deal-by-deal basis. 'Good' is not just defined as financially rewarding, but satisfying: the investor can really make a difference to the company into which he or she is buying.

David Giampaolo

David Giampaolo previously founded, built up and sold several businesses and health club chains in the US and UK. In 2002 he led a management buy-in of Pi Capital and became the CEO and a major shareholder.

He remains active in several other business interests, including having played a leading role in assisting BC Partners in their September 2005 buy-out of Fitness First, the world's largest health and fitness group. He remains on the Board of Directors of Fitness First and numerous other UK and US companies.

www.picapital.co.uk

This seems to be how wealthy people really enjoy themselves, by actually still doing things in a business context. They have to learn not to be too 'hands-on' as this will inevitably lead to conflict with the entrepreneurs. But they can still be involved in their own way. It could be improving the systems of the business, suggesting potential executives from their personal networks, setting up deals with their high-profile contacts — whatever they personally most enjoy doing.

This is exactly the kind of 'angel' investor an entrepreneur needs; someone who will take an active interest in the business, rather than turn up once month for a board meeting in search of the return on their cash.

If you are missing your profit forecasts, then you probably have a Sales Director or a Finance Director out of their depth (or both). If this is one of your co-founders, then the issue is personal as well as business-related. An external investor with real hands-on experience will usually have experience of 'letting go' someone who they were close to, so can advise on the best way to do it.

External investors also provide a necessary check and balance for the business itself. Most entrepreneurs want to have fun first and make money second; an angel investor will understand this and keep this under control.

The ideal investor sticks with an entrepreneur, preventing them from getting carried away with unrealistic ideas but at the same time keeping their enthusiasm alive (and focused on the core business, where it belongs). They truly merit the term 'angel'.

Rescue Remedy

Financial Times, 25th April 2009

In these difficult times it is useful to remember the lessons of the last recession of 1991.

Keith Steven not only remembers 1991; the events of that time are the 'defining experience' that drove him to create his current business.

He was running a retail chain but the company became over-extended and he found himself at loggerheads with his various landlords and the bank. The company was put into receivership.

Looking back, he concluded that he had not been offered the full range of options when the company got into trouble. He resolved to use his own experience to help others in this situation and formed KSA Turnaround, which specialises in company rescue.

> "Understand when you need help, the earlier the better"

Dealing with entrepreneurs, I am often reminded of Mr Micawber from David Copperfield, who was always convinced 'something will turn up'. For entrepreneurs, this is typically a big order that has been on the horizon for some time. When this fails to materialise, optimism turns instantly to despair. Mr Micawber was always being pursued by his creditors.

The challenge is to understand when you need help, the earlier the better. A good exercise is to re-examine your management accounts and put in the assumption that 25% of your predicted revenue just goes away and your largest customer suddenly decides to buy from one of your most aggressive competitors. Then assume your biggest suppliers will no longer be so flexible on payment and then look at the 'spikes' in your cash flow, the times when payroll and taxes have to be paid.

This is not an easy exercise for many entrepreneurs, who a) are optimists by nature and b) often dislike the minutiae of finance

this is how **yoodoo** it.

(even of finance actualities, let alone 'what-if' financial exercises). But it is worth doing.

Warned in advance, Keith and his team of company rescuers can get to work. Terms of leases can be renegotiated. Landlords commonly ask for a year's rent in advance, terms you were willing to accept just after that funding round.

Your moving to a monthly payment scheme will have a radical effect on your cash-flow and may even save your company. Landlords don't want tenants defaulting on their lease any more than you want to go bankrupt.

This approach, based on a sensible dialogue with both parties' interests at heart, can be extended to all your creditors. This includes your suppliers, the bank and even the tax authorities, who can be very reasonable if you approach them correctly.

But this negotiation should be done on your behalf by people like Keith, who have not only made an honest appraisal of your business, but also speak the language that your creditors understand.

Keith Steven

Keith Steven is a turnaround management expert, developing leading-edge turnaround strategies and delivering innovative rescue solutions.

He developed the UK's first on-line support website for struggling business.

www.companyrescue.co.uk

Ideally, a company rescue is done in good time to prevent, rather than treat, the disease. A Company Voluntary Arrangement (CVA) is a deal between the company and its creditors to repay them from future profits or by selling some of the assets of the business.

In this situation the directors remain in control of the company, personal guarantees do not usually get called in and it gives the business a fighting chance to survive. The CVA process stops pressure from tax, VAT and PAYE, and you can potentially use the instrument to terminate employment contracts, onerous supply contracts and even leases if this is what is required to restructure the company into profitability.

Even the sensible approach of a CVA can be a bitter blow for entrepreneurs. Another aim of KSA is to ensure that they emerge from the process with not just some self-respect, but also their family home, marriage and sanity intact. An entrepreneur himself at heart, Keith Steven is prouder of this aspect of his work than any other.

Part Five:

Building the Team

Though a lot of high-profile entrepreneurs won't admit it, entrepreneurship is a team game.

I begin this section with a piece by Kelvin McKenzie on life as a cornerstone for one of the most successful entrepreneurs of our time, Rupert Murdoch. Two pieces follow on different aspects of 'cornerstoneship' — the foil, and a piece of wisdom from entrepreneur Spencer Gallagher: hire people brighter than yourself.

I also look at what can go wrong with the entrepreneur/cornerstone relationship, and what to do if it does. Finally, there are three pieces on leadership.

Paul Bridle approaches the subject from a research perspective: start with an open mind, and find out what actually works. Allan Leighton has led two large organisations with a national profile, ASDA and the Post Office. And Philip Trousdell (or Lt Gen Sir Philip Trousdell, KBE, CBE, to give him his full title) has led in arguably the most successful and longest-lasting organisation in the whole country, the British Army.

Is The Boss Always Right?

Financial Times, 2nd February 2008

One attribute that well describes many entrepreneurs is 'being right about everything', a delicate mix of supreme confidence and impossible arrogance.

This is another way of describing the important prerequisite for anyone starting a new business: the need for total self-belief. However good your idea, there are always plenty of people who will question your ability to deliver: this quite rightly enrages entrepreneurs, as it is always much easier to pick holes in a new business idea than actually to get off your backside and start a company.

But another key entrepreneur attribute is 'not seeing the wood for the trees'; common sense and perspective can go out of the window in the white heat of enthusiasm for a new venture.

> "The best entrepreneurs hire people at least as effective and opinionated as themselves"

In The Beermat Entrepreneur I stressed the need for the entrepreneur to listen to the good advice of mentors, to delegate key tasks to top-quality 'cornerstones' and then not interfere unnecessarily. The best entrepreneurs realise this, and hire people at least as effective and opinionated as themselves. This can be a volatile combination.

Step forward Kelvin MacKenzie, former editor of The Sun, who worked closely with Rupert Murdoch, one of the world's most successful entrepreneurs.

It is difficult to imagine a higher-pressure job than editing a Fleet Street tabloid, having to both satisfy a highly motivated proprietor and entertain and inform a large readership on a daily basis, with the government of the day in the middle somewhere eager to rope you into their agenda.

Of course, it was not all plain sailing. Kelvin told me the story of having to send a fax to Rupert Murdoch explaining that they had finally looked at all the evidence and they would indeed have to pay Elton John's lawyers £1million.

This resulted in an industrial-strength 20-minute phone call from the proprietor, leaving the editor wondering why he had not been fired. (The reason was that Murdoch clearly felt Kelvin was still the right man for the job, despite this particular slip-up.)

Cornerstones know they will inevitably have to stand up to the entrepreneur sooner or later. The entrepreneur should have the wisdom to accept this confrontation, judge it on its merits, and, when appropriate, take the advice on board, for the greater good of the business. The experienced cornerstone also knows to take it in good grace when their good idea is later claimed by the entrepreneur as their own.

Large companies pack their boards with experienced non-executive directors to add a wider perspective and, if necessary, mediate between the Chief Executive and their operational team. In smaller companies egos can take over, resulting in a spiral of confrontation and counter-claims, which can be very destructive, if not actually fatal, to the enterprise.

> Kelvin was inspired by Rupert Murdoch to become an entrepreneur himself

Everyone working for a powerful entrepreneur has an array of colourful anecdotes to share with family and friends.

A typical audience response is to query why they still work for such an irrational martinet, with an underlying suspicion that perhaps they do it because they actually secretly enjoy the mood swings and abuse.

My experience is that cornerstones work for entrepreneurs because they find them inspiring. Kelvin was inspired by Rupert Murdoch to become an entrepreneur himself. After leaving The

Sun, he had mixed success with L!veTV, but later turned around Talk Radio which was eventually sold for a tidy sum.

Today Kelvin is working on his next entrepreneurial venture but remains a columnist at his spiritual home, The Sun. He considers he always understood the views and aspirations of the typical Sun reader and still clearly enjoys giving voice to them; a recent column resulted in thousands of e-mails suggesting he should be Prime Minister.

Kelvin Mackenzie

Kelvin Mackenzie was editor of The Sun from 1981 to 1994. He then joined BSkyB, followed by three years as MD of L!ve TV. He went on to found Talksport, the commercial radio station. Today he writes a weekly column for The Sun and is chairman of a video technology business.

A Great Double Act

Financial Times, 5th April 2008

We are all familiar with the great double acts in popular culture.

Great examples include Morecambe and Wise, Lennon and McCartney, even Del-Boy and Rodney; complementary characters who play off each other's strengths so that the 'whole' of their co-operative venture is greater than the sum of its parts.

Business is exactly the same. Sole trader Michael Marks joined forces with Thomas Spencer in Leeds' Kirkgate market; salesman Charles Rolls met engineer Henry Royce and started a car company; more recently Charles Dunstone and David Ross co-founded Carphone Warehouse.

This is a very successful model, and I always advise that entrepreneurs looking to develop beyond being a sole trader should find a 'foil', someone who shares the vision but who has a complementary set of business skills.

This should be someone with whom who they immediately click, sharing common views on Life, The Universe and Everything, as illustrated by creator Douglas Adams and John Lloyd, producer of the original radio version of The Hitchhiker's Guide to the Galaxy.

At the same time, the double act should ideally feature complementary personalities; if one is extrovert, the other should be introvert; someone good at starting things should find an expert finisher; if you are no good with figures find someone who is.

A common division of labour in a double act is for one person to drum up the vital early sales and the other to concentrate on delivering the product or service. But as the company develops the edges get blurred, and successful partnerships develop a more in-depth understanding, where both find themselves able to do the other person's job when required.

This is perfectly illustrated by Lindsey Walker and Shelley-Anne Salisbury, the team behind the very successful 'Linziclip'. This is a revolutionary new hair clip which, due to its patented advanced gripping mechanism and two-spring device, camouflages and hides the inner workings of the old style butterfly clip whilst holding the hair more effectively.

Lindsey may have an inventor's DNA; her grandfather invented an insulating blanket for aero engines in the First World War. One of her first inventions was a fabulous hairpiece, but, like many inventors, she found herself being copied and her patent infringed but did not have the expertise to pursue the matter through the courts.

She then had a chance meeting with Shelley-Anne, a successful corporate lawyer. Their partnership developed as they discussed something that annoyed them both: butterfly clips that were both ungainly and uncomfortable. Several prototypes were made in the Blue Peter style from toilet rolls and glitter, and they eventually developed the Linziclip, which was immediately patented as widely as possible.

> "Find a 'foil', someone who shares the vision but who has a complementary set of business skills"

It took a little while to establish credibility, especially with manufacturers in India who were expecting a Mr Walker and a Mr Salisbury. But the invention was neat and practicable, and they had the business skills to develop it from prototype into final manufacture. Linziclips are now available in 17 countries, including over 20,000 outlets in the USA.

When talking to Lindsey and Shelley-Anne, it is impossible to pigeonhole one or either of them into any particular business category. Both are equally adept at any aspect of the business, be it improving the design of the Linziclips or protecting their intellectual property.

They seem telepathic almost to the point of completing each other's sentences, and while they have robust discussions about how to develop the business, they always seem to find a resolution, as they share such a common vision for its direction.

The message for entrepreneurs is that the success of your business is not just about the merits of your idea; it is about your ability to find this 'foil', someone who can help you turn your good idea into a great business. As challenges arise, a problem shared is a problem more than halved, and, as opportunities develop, you can study them together and decide if they are right for your business.

There is also something to be learned from the great show business double acts. Morecambe and Wise were successful because of their extraordinary comedic skills and personal chemistry on stage, even though they rarely met socially. But if a business opportunity arose, they would turn it down unless both of them felt comfortable with the deal — excellent advice for business double acts.

Shelley-Anne Salisbury and Lindsey Walker

After meeting at a party and realising that they had a meeting of minds, Shelley-Anne Salisbury and Lindsey Walker joined forces and set up Linshell Innovations Ltd. Following a 'eureka' moment while they were trying to pin back their hair with a butterfly clip, they set about completely re-inventing this traditional clamp or claw clip which is worn by almost everyone with long hair.

The Linziclip® is now sold in 17 countries worldwide. In the US and Canada, the Linziclip® is available in 20,000 stores such as RiteAid, CVS, Walgreens and Sally Beauty. Other retail outlets selling the Linziclip® around the world include Boots, Claire's Accessories, AS Watson, Ahold and Schlecker.

Scaling up

Financial Times, 23rd February 2008

It is hard setting up a new business. It is even harder scaling it up.

This inevitably requires the entrepreneur to hire people better than themselves. This requires both courage and humility. Entrepreneurs usually have plenty of the former, but can be a bit short of the latter.

Anyone starting a business has to be versatile. They have to have enough sales ability to secure some customers; then they have to be able to deliver on their promises, often working long hours; finally, they have to do their own finances.

This can be very hard work and explains why a large number of businesses run out of steam in the first year. But if you are successful, you can then start scaling.

I discussed this process with Spencer Gallagher, who stumbled into web design after a career in clothing retail. He had early success with his company Bluhalo doing simple websites for start-ups; his bright idea was to trawl the database at Companies House for newly registered businesses and offer them a quick 'get up and running' service.

"It was time to hire people to do the jobs he hated the most"

Business was good and they were able to expand, so Spencer realised it was time to hire people do the jobs he hated the most. Top of the list was finance.

Spencer approached the job of finding a Finance Cornerstone in exactly the right way. It had to be someone who Spencer liked, and who understood and agreed with the direction he wanted to take Bluhalo. He then told this person that they also had to pay their way as soon as possible, to cover their salary and more with increased profits.

The new financial rigour introduced by this person was not always popular — with the rest of the team, or with Spencer

this is how **yoodoo** it.

himself, who had to submit to it. The natural mode of the entrepreneur is to say 'yes' to members of staff, which can lead to a lax regime for personal expenses. It is very common for a new Finance Cornerstone to attract the nickname 'Dr No', but increased awareness of the need to control costs is a natural part of the growing-up process for any small company.

The next expert that Spencer hired was an experienced project manager from IBM. Small companies usually deliver projects by the proverbial 'seat of the pants'; this works for a small number of customers, but scaling this up is very hard. It requires skills that can only be gained from the successful delivery of large projects, skills most often found in large organisations.

This project manager was again given the specific brief of saving her own salary and more. She used the project management methodology they used at IBM, which turned out not to be as monolithic or inflexible as Spencer had first feared.

Spencer Gallagher

Like many successful entrepreneurs, Spencer Gallagher left school at 16 with no qualifications. His entrepreneurial spirit built him a successful career until, armed with only £4,500 redundancy, he formed Bluhalo, which was acquired by Gyro International in 1998.

This enabled Bluhalo to raise themselves from the hundreds of thousands of companies who offer web design to one of the most successful in the country. Bluhalo now specialise in large sports sites. These have large numbers of visitors looking at increasing amounts of ever-changing content. This requires advanced software development skills as well as expert customer management — all skills that Spencer has brought into the company.

Taking on people like this enables the entrepreneur to back off from management and to spend more time turning the next good idea into a great business, which is what many of us are best at. It is, in a way, a recipe for eternal youth: perhaps the best role model for the aspiring entrepreneur is not Richard Branson or Bill Gates, but Peter Pan.

The Case of the Clashing Cornerstone

Financial Times, 10th November 2007

Eric Edmeades is a self-made millionaire and CEO of a computer-based special effects company.

But he started as a 'cornerstone' to an entrepreneur. They then fell out, prompting Eric to start his own business — very successfully.

I know exactly how he felt; I've been in exactly the same position and witnessed this happen in many other start-ups. This is bad news for the entrepreneur: their ability to grow past sole trader status is entirely dependent on their ability to attract and retain 'cornerstones'.

'Cornerstones' is the special term in the Beermat model to describe the most important people in the start-up business. They complement the entrepreneur's vision and drive with practical skills, making sure the three main areas — sales, delivery and finance — are covered.

I recommend strongly that, once they have proved their worth, cornerstones be given a stake in the business so they have tangible as well as emotional 'skin in the game'. Entrepreneurs often find it easy to attract potential cornerstones; the real problem is in retaining them.

> "Cornerstones... are the most important people in the start-up business"

The early days in a start-up are characterised by frantic work, euphoria and many, many promises. There are not just promises to customers about delivery and quality but also promises to the cornerstones about future wealth and happiness: bonuses, stock options and even actual shares. These should be documented (the Finance Cornerstone is the person to do this).

Eric Edmeades

Eric Edmeades is the CEO of the Kerner Companies, a spin-off of George Lucas' Industrial Light and Magic and a world leader in physical effects, models, pyrotechnics and 3D technologies.

Before joining Kerner, Eric founded the ITR Group, an integrator and maintainer of wireless networking and mobile computing technologies. He sold the business in 2005 and became a sought-after international speaker and business consultant. Eric is also passionate about nature conservation, wildlife photography and disaster relief work.

www.ericedmeades.com

Over time, splits in the top team can develop. It takes two to make a dispute, and it's never entirely the fault of one party. Like any divorce, there will be counter-claims and mud-slinging, with many arguments about money, though this is the symptom of the problem rather than the root cause, the 'sneeze' as opposed to the 'influenza'.

If you talk to the cornerstone, it's all about the entrepreneur's unreasonable behaviour, of new people coming in being offered preferential status and better stock options, and a nostalgia for the 'good old days' when everyone knew what was going on, and they personally felt more loved and respected than they do now.

If you speak to the entrepreneur, you hear stories of the cornerstone no longer pulling their weight, of not understanding the wider picture and their own pressures 'at the top'. The cornerstones should understand that things have moved on since those early, simpler days.

First port of call in these cases should be the company's

mentors, typically people who have seen it all before. They can moderate in a dispute between two aggrieved parties, ideally creating a consensus.

If this fails, the only solution is a civilized divorce, ideally with generous terms for the cornerstone, as a mark of respect for the contribution they made in the early stages of the business, when success was by no means assured.

Eric Edmeades' departure from his company was not like this. Looking back, he actually feels grateful this happened: it spurred him to success. The loser was the person who thought they had won, his old boss. So if you are an entrepreneur, respect your cornerstones and work with them. And if you are a cornerstone who has not been well-treated and has instead been pushed out of the business you helped found, remember the old adage, 'the best revenge is a happy life'. Eric is an excellent example of that.

'Leadership Methodology'

Financial Times, 17th May 2008

There has been much focus on the leadership abilities of our politicians.

Jacqui Smith resigned as Home Secretary and implied she might have been better trained for the role. In London we have seen a seasoned politician replaced by someone with undoubted charm and intelligence but little hands-on experience of government. Will Boris Johnson make a great Mayor of London?

I decided to consult a subject matter expert, Paul Bridle, who has made a long study of leadership in effective organisations: what actually works and what doesn't.

Sadly for David Brent and other would-be office comedians, 'a sense of humour' does not feature highly in the list of what people seek in a leader.

> "What people look for most is a vision, a clear statement of where the organisation is going"

Instead, Paul has found out that what people look for most is a vision, a clear statement of where the organisation is going. This is relatively easy for most politicians; there are manifesto promises carefully thought out in advance of the campaign, even if they may have to be modified later.

The second quality is that team members know exactly where they stand with the leader. This is a common problem for entrepreneurs as their company grows. The early people are fundamental in the design and execution of the original vision.

As the numbers of staff increase, new employees can become 'flavour of the month', much to the distress of the original cornerstones. The entrepreneur having mood swings as their responsibilities and stress increase can aggravate this fickleness.

this is how **yoodoo** it.

Paul explains that successful leadership is not about leaders making sure that people like them, but they do need to be open and predictable in their behaviour. They should treat staff — and customers — in the way they would like to be treated themselves.

Employees should feel valued and that their achievements are recognised. There are many ways to do this, including a monthly company get-together with awards for the best-performing people. I have always felt that the most interesting company award is for 'unsung hero', someone who has over-delivered even though they are out of the limelight.

Willingness to learn is a third key leadership attribute. Some people are great natural leaders, but even for them, there are always best practices to learn from other people's experiences. The wise leader realises that they are a never-ending journey of continuous personal development, and arranges regular training for themselves.

Finally, Paul mentions the most difficult facet of successful leadership: the

Paul Bridle

Paul Bridle is a Leadership Methodologist. For nearly two decades he has researched effective organisations and the people that lead them. As a result of his work he has been voted 12th in the Top 30 Most Influential Leadership Gurus in the World in 2007 & 2008.

As a result of his research around the world, he is called upon to assist both private as well as public organisations by acting as an advisor or consultant on a range of projects relating to management and leadership issues or development.

Paul spends approximately 25% of his year carrying out research into effective organisations and the people that lead them. He is the author of two books and writes articles for magazines and journals around the world.

www.paulbridle.com

ability to let go. It starts with hiring people cleverer than you and then moves onto handing over completely when the time is right. This is an area that many entrepreneurs find difficult, even ones who in theory have thought out a clear 'exit strategy'.

In politics, exits are almost always painful, as Margaret Thatcher and Gordon Brown have found. Let's hope that Boris Johnson makes a great Mayor of London, with a clear vision and staff and constituents who know where they stand. He should be a man of the people who recognises achievements in others, but who is always willing to learn. And when his time finally comes, let us hope he is able to make a dignified and orderly exit.

Doing the Right Thing

Daily Telegraph, September 2007

"Leadership isn't a popularity contest."

I'm listening to Allan Leighton, Chairman of Royal Mail. He's certainly taken on a classic leadership challenge, judging by the current press coverage of industrial action and concerns over Post Office closures.

He also released a book On Leadership — Practical Wisdom from the People That Know, a compendium of advice from Allan and some of his friends, including Rupert Murdoch, Philip Green and James Dyson.

So why a book on leadership? "I've read lots of books on management and leadership," says Allan, "and found more and more of them are being written by people who've never managed or led anything. You think 'that's difficult', when actually in my experience it's largely common sense."

Allan is a great believer in simplicity: "I've always felt if you can't say anything in 20 minutes, then the chances of anybody else being able to get it is very low."

Allan is clearly not a fan of the academic approach to business, given his 18-year apprenticeship at 'The University of Life', or more specifically, Mars. He was first attracted to the company by the promise of a car and a belief in his ability to sell Mars bars.

He still remembers the company acronym: F.E.M.R.Q., which stands for Freedom, Efficiency, Mutuality, Responsibility and Quality, remembered as 'Forest E. Mars Requires Quality'. He was very happy at Mars, and might still be there now, had not the inevitable head-hunter called with an opportunity too good to miss...

"Asda was the first superstore business in the UK, very focused on what they were trying to do. And then, as always happens, the team changed, new people came in and instead of sticking to the knitting, they got into all sorts of other things. The core business started to dissipate, and when we went in it was worth £500 million and they had billions of debt.

Leaving Mars was a very tough decision, 51%-49%. But in many ways those are the best ones; they are the ones you really think about. So off I went. I was at Asda for 10 years, the last 4 or 5 as the CEO. It was fantastic because it was so bad we could try anything.

Naivety is great because you try things that other people wouldn't, but you actually get them to work. Half of the stuff didn't work and 50% of the stuff did; over time we just built a pattern."

Eventually Asda was sold to Wal-Mart, a company whose best ideas he had been happily stealing for some time. "I used to go out there, see what they were doing, copy their ideas and get arrested in the stores for taking photographs. They let me off when they knew who I was."

It was time to move on: Allan took a number of directorships, including what was then Consignia. One of his first actions was to change the name back to the Royal Mail, for the most traditional of reasons: "I am very proud to be British and here is something that has been around Britain for 200 years. Not many things have 'Royal' attached; it's part of the country. Every day one of our people walks down somebody's path and puts a letter through the door; there is a great deal of heritage.

> "Tough decisions… are the best ones. They are the ones you really think about"

I did the job for three or four months and just fell in love with it, which seems odd as we were in the middle of a national strike. The business was financially in a very bad shape; the whole market was about to be opened up to competition and we were highly regulated. It could have gone seriously wrong, but I thought, well, here is another thing to turn around.

There is a lot to change and change is difficult for people to stomach sometimes. But the whole leadership thing is about doing the right thing. You can't kid yourself. We are trying to create something that is really sustainable.

this is how **yoodoo** it.

I keep saying I am not bothered about where we are in 5 minutes or 5 weeks or 5 months but where we are in 5 years, because that's what my job is, to create something that's sustainable over time. And unless we do this, we will be in much more trouble then than we are now."

He then outlined his vision of that future: "I think we will have a much more vibrant Post Office. There is always talk about closures, and it is very difficult, because we don't own them; individuals own Post Offices and Post Offices close because individuals can't generate a living.

But I think 95% of the population will have a Post Office within a mile. However, it will be a very different Post Office, much more banking and insurance related. We already have a 40% market share in the foreign exchange market; we created that in the last 6 years."

Putting his leadership book together helped concentrate his mind on what is required for such a challenge: "You have to be very focused, by which I mean have a clear vision and be unrelenting in pursuit of it.

But you also have to be a very good listener; it is very important to understand how people think about things, even if they think differently to you. And the third essential is to keep everything very simple. Focus, listen, keep it simple: if you just do those three things, then life is a breeze for everybody."

Finally, the conversation moves onto fun, a key element in his book. He writes in glowing terms about a dispute solved at South West Airlines by arm-wrestling, and tells stories of his people at Asda dressing up as bananas. He is convinced that people are more productive and efficient when they're having fun.

"I was out in Canada and we got these sumo wrestling suits; that was good fun — although it's quite difficult when you are lying on your back and you can't get up. It doesn't mean that you are not professional; you can be fun and professional as opposed to serious and professional."

Allan Leighton is clearly fun to work with, even if he has to make difficult decisions and negotiate hard when he feels it is right. It was reported that the Royal Mail unions would only resume talks at a particularly difficult impasse if Allan himself came to the table. I'm sure the negotiations were fun and professional, even if he wasn't the most popular man in the room at the time.

Allan Leighton

Allan Leighton started his career in Mars Confectionery as a Salesman in 1974. He worked his way up through the company before leaving in 1991. He then joined Pedigree Petfoods, where he was Sales Director until his appointment in 1992 to Asda Stores Ltd.

He began his career in Asda as Group Marketing Director and was appointed Chief Executive in September 1996. In November 1999 when the American company Wal-Mart bought Asda, Allan became the President and CEO of Wal-Mart Europe.

In November 2000 he left Asda and was later Chairman of Royal Mail Group plc, President of Loblaw Companies Ltd, Deputy Chairman of Selfridges & Co and George Weston Ltd and Non-Executive Director of BSkyB Group plc.

Leadership, Army-style

Daily Telegraph, **Tuesday 28th August 2007**

"Ask good questions, listen carefully and give clear instructions."

Sound advice indeed, and I'm writing it down carefully as I'm talking to Sir Philip Trousdell, formerly director of the multinational NATO force in Bosnia and commander of the operation in Northern Ireland. He's telling me about his take on leadership, Army-style.

Like many very senior military figures, Sir Philip has a keen intellect, urbane charm and dry wit, but underneath you sense someone with a very refined sense of purpose, who doesn't suffer fools gladly.

He makes a clear distinction between management, which he says is about getting everything organised properly, and leadership, which is about taking people further than they think they can go. He bases his views on leadership on the classic Army experience: every 3 years or so, you're pitched into a new command. As well as the jobs I've already listed, he was also director of public relations for the Army and commanded 48th Gurkha Brigade in Hong Kong.

In one job, he had to deal with the tabloid press, and in the other he managed a highly multi-cultural environment, two challenges that would terrify even the best-prepared chief executive.

It all started for him at the Royal Military Academy, Sandhurst, in the '60s. Even then, the Academy was in the forefront of psychometric training, which Sir Philip says was 'pretty accurate', using the technique to select the next batch of officers.

The training was backed up by very structured interviewing ('you have to eyeball them over the table'), and followed by academic study featuring one of the best history libraries in the world, and 'a significant time running around in the mud'.

He tells me that while at the Sovereign's Parade you see people who look absolutely identical in their uniform and behave identically on the drill square, "actually that's not what we select them for. We select them for their ability to think their way through a situation."

Then these fledgling leaders get their first command, in his case a platoon of 30 men in the middle of the Libyan Desert. It is at this point that all young officers learn an important lesson: however strong a leader they think they are, the unit is actually run by the Sergeant Major. Hence the first two of Sir Philip's key leadership skills, the ability to ask good questions and to listen to the replies.

> "Communication is an absolute skill. If you can't communicate I don't think you should be in the leadership business"

Back in the '90s, I remember everyone becoming very excited by 'upwards appraisal', where you review your boss. Today, '360 degree reviews' are much vaunted. It seems the Army has always been ahead of the game.

Sir Philip says: "People often say about the Army, that you only ever get reported on by your superiors. But if you go and have dinner in the Sergeant's mess then you had better leave your pompousness at the door and put on your humility hat because, very kindly and politely, these guys, who may be 4 or 5 years older than you, tell you exactly how it's working."

"If you listen to them, they tell you a huge amount. But if you aren't listening hard then you miss it. Particularly if you are not in a position to read their body language as well — that's a really hard lesson to learn."

Finally, you need to make your decisions and explain them clearly.

"Communication is an absolute skill. If you can't communicate I don't think you should be in the leadership business," he says.

"You need to be able to articulate unambiguously and clearly to the people who are going to implement the decision, so that they have no doubts about what's going on."

"And then you need to start wearing out the shoe leather, going around all the levels of your organisation, explaining where they fit in, what their part is in this great scheme that you've dreamt up, so that they not only understand what's required but also have the chance to ask you questions."

So there is leadership, Army-style: 'question', 'listen' and 'communicate'. If you're having leadership problems in your new, growing organisation, learn from one that has hundreds of years' experience and go back to basics for some training in these simple but essential life skills. ▪

Sir Philip Trousdell

Sir Philip Trousdell left the Army as a member of the Army Board in 2005. His second career has focussed on leadership development. He has been the Chairman of an IT development company, worked in international pharmaceuticals and is currently Chairman of Corporate Battlefields which uses military leadership and management experience to enhance corporate effectiveness.

Part Six:

Mentors and Mentoring

'Get a mentor' was one of the main messages
of The Beermat Entrepreneur.

I'm delighted to see that the message has
really taken off, and mentoring is now a
key part of business support.

Here are some pieces on the subject; one
about getting the best from receiving
mentoring, another about how to give it,
and a third about business coaching, which
is subtly different to mentoring.

Coaches are not supposed to give
advice: the ethos of coaching assumes the
client (or 'coachee', a word that always
makes me think of tickling babies) has
all the knowledge inside them, and the
coach's job is to help them access this.
A mentor, on the other hand, is free to
advise, and is indeed expected to.

I conclude the section with a piece
on my own mentoring experience at the
Entrepreneur Business School in Bali.

Getting the Best from Your Mentor

Financial Times, 5th January 2008

We all have mentors, even if we do not realise it.

For people in school, it might be a teacher who is willing to spend a little extra time with you. It could be a family friend who always has good advice and contacts. For those of you still in the corporate world, dreaming of starting your own business, it is the person who might actually be able to make that happen.

The ground rules for mentoring are simple: you must like your mentor and they must like you. If this is the case, they will spare you some of their valuable time, always the most precious currency.

You should make it fun and easy for your mentor. It will be fun if you do your preparation and later act on the advice, and it will be easy if you pick a time and place that suits them.

I have worked in numerous start-ups and in one I received some fundamental mentoring from our chairman, Sir Campbell Fraser. He had been Chairman of Dunlop and Director-General of the CBI.

> "You must like your mentor and they must like you"

First of all, he made me simplify my description of the complex software system we were trying to sell. What problems did it solve, and who might actually need, and thus buy, it? It took me an embarrassingly long time to get this description into a form that satisfied him — but of course he was completely right.

He then picked up the phone to someone in senior management at British Telecom, as BT Group was then known, and effectively got us our first order.

This is perhaps the best thing a mentor can do for a start-up — but be cautious. Mentors are understandably protective of their personal networks, and you should always take this into consideration before randomly asking to be connected.

this is how **yoodoo** it.

In the corporate world, a good boss can be a mentor. He or she can advise you in your current work, but may also be prepared to discuss your new ideas, both in and outside the company. If you have an entrepreneurial idea, he or she can suggest that if it does not work out, you can always come back, better for having tried.

They might even suggest that the company be the first customer for your products, a win for both parties, which has bootstrapped many an early-stage entrepreneur.

I was discussing mentoring with René Carayol, the speaker and leadership expert, whose television credits include the series Pay Off Your Mortgage in Two Years. His business career has mostly been in large companies, and he still speaks fondly about his first break at Marks & Spencer, where his mentor was the group IT director.

This person is now retired, but René still meets him once a quarter. "I look forward to these meetings, with pleasure but also a touch of nerves," he says. "My mentor pulls no punches. He's direct and to the point, tough and explicit."

René Carayol

René Carayol is one of the world's leading business gurus focusing on leadership and culture, drawing from his experiences as a board member of some of the biggest British and American organisations. He is the best-selling author of the business bible 'Corporate Voodoo', a regular television and radio broadcaster and a Visiting Professor at Cass Business School. In 2004 René was awarded an MBE for outstanding service to the business community.

www.inspiredleaders.com

Mentors will stop you making elementary mistakes, René points out. They will have contacts which may be worth more than their weight in gold, plus they will have insights into the flaws in your character that you will be able to address by putting together the right team. They are hugely valuable.

I felt some envy for René, as Sir Campbell passed away last year. I have not found anyone to replace his combination of razor-sharp worldliness and gentle, self-deprecating charm. Maybe I never will — right now, I take mentoring from a number of people on different topics.

I am finding this helpful in a new way: there is more than one way to get the best out of mentoring. But Campbell always said we were friends, and that is what the best mentors become. ▧

Grown-Up Behaviour

Financial Times, 30th August 2008

The biggest challenge that any of us can face is not in the workplace, but at home: parenthood.

Suddenly, there is a noisy little bundle of joy who demands our total commitment and unconditional love, 24 hours a day, 7 days a week.

The challenge of starting a business is a close second, with eager anticipation followed by many sleepless nights and much metaphorical nappy changing. But just as a sensible new parent gets help from experienced family members and other experts, a wise entrepreneur seeks the advice of their mentors and even engages a business coach.

Nowadays, there is no stigma in hiring a business coach; the top sports people are coached every day as they are always looking for that extra edge in their very competitive environment, so why shouldn't business people be?

Even the simplest coaching can produce immediate results. Typical first tasks for an entrepreneur include setting realistic objectives and then putting them in some kind of order of priority – separating the wood from the trees. But the underlying reasons for a lack of perspective or poor performance may involve deeper issues which need to be to be examined further, which is where the coach's skill really comes to the fore.

Stephen Schneider has considerable experience in human resources, working at board level in several public companies and with Henley Management College, before starting CPS Ltd in 1996. His company provides coaching and mentoring for senior executives who suddenly find themselves out of their depth.

The challenges people face in a new role appear to be about new tasks, but Stephen explains that fundamentally the problems are about the person themselves and how well they are psychologically equipped to deal with their new responsibilities.

A common problem is dealing with a strong authority figure. This is aggravated if the new taker of responsibility has had issues with their own parents, who may have died when they were young or have been largely absent when they were growing up.

Stephen also talks of 'envy pre-emption', when a client finds themselves under-achieving through feelings of guilt at out-shining their parents. They may be the first in their family to go to university, or feel uncomfortable that they have higher earnings and better opportunities than their parents.

> Typical first tasks for an entrepreneur include setting realistic objectives and then putting them in some kind of order of priority

This can lead to a lack of willingness to perform to their maximum potential if they find themselves confronted by a strong character in the boardroom, despite excellent credentials for getting there in the first place.

Another problem can be an authoritarian style. Despite the liberal tone of much HR material, this can work well in some management roles. It does not work well when someone joins a board, which is an essentially collaborative entity.

A good board member has to show expertise in advocacy, which Stephen defines as being the ability to hear all the evidence, come to sensible conclusions and then provide clear recommendations.

The techniques that Stephen and his colleagues use to address the challenges of joining a boardroom are just as important for a small business. All entrepreneurs should consider asking for professional help, especially when the company itself crosses that line between a 'start-up' (a 'sapling', in our Beermat terminology) and a fully-fledged company.

In The Beermat Entrepreneur, I said this happens when the firm consists of around 20 or so people: Stephen is much more specific — the magic number is 32.

Entrepreneurs are usually complex and driven people, and this is often due to their having had issues with their parents. So it is ironic that when these entrepreneurs become successful they suddenly find themselves in loco parentis, acting as a mother or father figure to their members of staff, who can be more demanding than real children at times.

If this irony becomes too painful, coaching can make a real difference. The message is clear: you should never be too proud to ask for help. ▨

Stephen Schneider

Since founding CPS in 1996, Stephen Schneider has built a reputation as a mentor and coach to boardroom directors and senior executives of some of the country's leading organisations.

Drawing on his extensive business career, his experience of psychoanalysis and his work with the Tavistock Institute and Henley Management College, Stephen has created an organisation that offers clients access to some of the UK's most experienced practitioners from the worlds of business and psychology.

Stephen's corporate background includes senior executive roles in ENSERCH Corporation of Dallas and Higgs & Hill where he was a member of the plc board. Today, as a member of Henley's Associate Faculty, he continues to facilitate groups regularly on their highly acclaimed experiential programme, Developing Leaders, and contributes regular articles and interviews on leadership and boardroom development to professional journals, the national press and radio.

www.cps-ltd.co.uk

Sending down the elevator

Financial Times, 3rd January 2009

One of my most challenging activities is providing mentoring to people who have just sold their companies.

They have gone from poor to rich in an instant, and the euphoria of the transaction has now been replaced with a distinct sense of anti-climax. Some of their friends, driven by envy, now dislike them; others are bombarding them with suggestions for investments or charitable causes. The result is fatigue, often allied with a vague sense of guilt.

My advice is always to not invest in anything in the short term and instead take a very long holiday. They should spend their new free time looking inwards at the person they have become and try to come to terms with their new position in society.

Many entrepreneurs feel the need to start a new venture right away, to prove they can do it again. This can be a big mistake, as they are often still damaged by the experience of the sale, a process often compared with suffering bereavement.

"Mentoring should always be given without any expectation of financial reward"

If they survive the process unscathed with a good perspective on their own weaknesses as well as their successes, then they have the raw material to become a mentor themselves. If this is of interest and they feel that they would enjoy the process, I then provide them with some practical tools.

I believe that mentoring should always be for free. It is entirely legitimate to charge for advice, but that is consultancy, a completely different business model, whose value for money should always be precisely measured. I believe strongly that mentoring should always be given without any expectation of financial reward, and therefore unbiased by any commercial considerations.

I have developed a precise system that seems to work well. I offer free one-hour sessions at short notice in a Central London location, filling in gaps between my other, paid work.

this is how yoodoo it.

I ask the person being mentored to first read The Beermat Entrepreneur, so they have an understanding of my model and do not require me to regurgitate large sections of the book.

I then ask them to invest $100 in their own personal development and complete an on-line psychometric test specifically designed for entrepreneurs, called Wealth Dynamics, devised by my good friend and social entrepreneur Roger Hamilton.

The Wealth Dynamics system helps me get a clear insight into their potential and personality, based on their match with the eight different profiles. (Memo to any cynics — no, I don't get any kickback from the Wealth Dynamics people. I genuinely believe this is a great self- understanding tool.)

Finally, I ask them to provide just one page on where they are and where they want to get to, rather than a detailed business plan or sheaves of marketing material. Some people sadly cannot summon the discipline to generate a concise one-pager, which probably means they are unlikely to make a successful career from entrepreneurship, at least for now.

Those who do the preparation correctly then get a totally focused hour of my time, and simple suggestions for the next steps they should take, as well as a promise to see them again if they pass this next small hurdle. They all seem to enjoy the process, as do I.

The key to successful mentoring is that it should be fun and a learning experience for both parties. As actor Kevin Spacey said, "When you have success, it's great to be able to send the elevator down for somebody else".

Roger Hamilton

Roger Hamilton is the creator of Wealth Dynamics, a social entrepreneur, author, speaker and dad.

Wealth Dynamics can be found at **http://wdprofiletest.com**

Healthy Optimism

Financial Times, 13th December 2008

I am always asking people for column ideas.

My editor's suggestion was to write something optimistic to counter the negative and cynical commentary currently rolling around the press, some even generated, sadly, by successful entrepreneurs.

Last week I was ideally placed to generate an upbeat column, as I was a mentor at the Entrepreneur Business School (EBS) Masters in Bali, organised and run by Roger Hamilton.

A regular EBS has 300 delegates and is a whirlwind adventure of learning, personal breakthroughs, connections with the universe, spontaneous disco dancing and compulsory hugging. Almost everyone leaves happy, motivated and with a renewed sense of purpose.

The Masters is a more concentrated affair, with only a handful of delegates and four mentors: me; Bob Urichuck, one of the best sales experts in the world; serial entrepreneur and executive master coach Martin Jimmink; and Roger Hamilton himself.

Our work as mentors was to drill deep into the delegates' value propositions, challenging them on exactly what their enterprise would provide and how they would deliver on their promises to their customers, their teams, their investors, themselves and finally to the world, to make it a better place. It was challenging stuff.

Delegates arrived from all over the world with a wide range of business ideas at different stages of development. Some, like Arabian Eye, a Dubai-based photo library, and IPS People, an Australian training company, had established businesses, which they were looking to take to the next level. Others came with no written-down business plan, and only a very general idea of what they wanted to do.

We mentors gave the best advice we could, based on what was put in front of us at each particular moment, at times a process similar to trying to nail jelly to a wall. We tried to resist the urge to intervene directly, as the purpose of the workshop was to let the delegates create systems that they could operate without expert help immediately to hand.

One delegate was clearly struggling; his business plan was creating little attraction from the group, and did not seem to be progressing much during the week. Roger then weaved his magic for the next 15 minutes, employing all the resources in the room to reposition the business idea into something clearly viable.

Roger even made a commitment to invest personally in the idea if the delegate were to take the recommended steps. The room was back to a high state of positivity, and the particular delegate had a clear road map for success.

Everyone left the workshop full of optimism and felt they had received outstanding value for money from what is not a cheap workshop, especially if you factor in the travel cost to Bali. I reflected with Roger on the events of the week, and we agreed that one of the hardest aspects of mentoring is that some delegates will not, for whatever reason, use the simple tools and clear instructions they received, and be no further ahead in 6 months' time.

Some people use EBS just as an adrenaline rush to feel good about themselves. Others are much more cynical and dismiss the event entirely, put off by the open displays of emotion and relentless optimism of their events. But EBS is attended by some very experienced business people, who use the event to establish new perspectives, and work out not just what they should do, but also who to do it with, when to do it, exactly how to do it, and, most importantly, why they should bother in the first place.

If they answer all these questions, they should be successful entrepreneurs. ▨

The author with (from left) Bob Urichuck, Roger Hamilton, Martin Jimmink, Bruce Muzik and Dave Rogers at an Entrepreneur Business School in Bali.

Part Seven:

Growing the Business

You've got over all the standard start-up hurdles. The business is booming. You've never felt better about it!

It might just be time to leave. Growing a business requires a different skill-set to starting one, and there are professionals out there who are experts at this. Here are interviews with three such people, three 'grown-ups' who know how to turn your happy tribe into a successful machine.

Natural, entrepreneurial and responsible

Daily Telegraph, 23rd October 2007

Be natural, be entrepreneurial, and be responsible.

I'm listening to Jamie Mitchell, UK managing director of Innocent Drinks.

Jamie himself is clearly a natural; I first bumped into him in the mid-90s when he was running an event at his Oxford college and I was touring a 70s show. Most professional bands dread playing Oxbridge May Balls, which are often run by arrogant unprofessional upstarts. He looked after us well and his event ran like clockwork: I thought this young man would go far...

He was quickly snapped up by McKinsey and found himself in Paris working on Häagen-Dazs' European strategy. After a couple of years he moved to the CBI, as bag-carrier and speech-writer to Adair Turner, the Director-General, followed by an MBA at Harvard Business School. The internet boom kicked in, and it seemed sensible to start a venture capital firm.

It was a great idea at the time. He would identify the best business plans and help them get funded, on a 'no raise, no fee' basis, providing around 25% of the investment. I was certainly sold on the idea and rushed in to help, having been involved in several successful start-ups. We had the time of our life and would probably still be there, had not the dot-com crash spoilt the fun.

We both licked our wounds and moved on. I decided to co-author The Beermat Entrepreneur with Chris West, extolling the virtues of building companies on revenue rather than perceived market valuation. Jamie started lecturing at London Business School, turning his hard experience into valuable learning. He did a case study on Innocent Drinks, and came to the attention of the founders. Naturally, they offered him a job, as Marketing Director. A year later he was UK Managing Director.

It was about 50 people when he joined, but soon grew to 220 people and £100 million turnover. The culture is phenomenal; people at Innocent are 'on a mission to prove that ethics and business aren't mutually exclusive'.

I was delighted to see Jamie, a former venture capitalist, now full of natural goodness: "The truth is I have been fascinated by business's responsibilities since my CBI days. It was really amazing to see a company actually trying to do it from the bottom up, rather than jumping on the bandwagon and saying: 'to protect our brand we'd better stick on some corporate social responsibility stuff'. Instead, here was a business founded on principles as opposed to purely on a profit motive."

> "People at Innocent are 'on a mission to prove that ethics and business aren't mutually exclusive'"

We then discussed the role of the new management in growing businesses. It's a common story: keen founders with a mission to change the world have some initial success, then, as the company grows, they realise they need 'grown-ups', people with proper management experience, to deal with the inevitable problems. Jamie, as one of these, found himself pitched in at the deep end.

"On my first day as UK Managing Director, one of our batches of strawberry and banana fizzed around a little bit and some of the tops came off. We ended up on a Watchdog programme."

This problem overcome, he set about putting in place some more structured business processes, closely measuring the success of TV campaigns and making sure some other 'grown-ups' were hired, including a Marketing Director from Cereal Partners.

So will Innocent Drinks ever change? Will the original founders sell out, like PJ Smoothies to Pepsi, or Ben and Jerry's to Unilever? They've had offers, of course, but... "The three founders are still young; they still enjoy every day at work. The business is growing, so value is being created. They feel they are making a difference in the world because of what this business does and how it does it. So in their mind, this is what they do: this is their baby, this is their life, this is their career."

So for now at least, it's business as usual, with no artificial ingredients: just being natural, entrepreneurial and responsible.

Jamie Mitchell

Jamie Mitchell has been starting up, investing in and managing entrepreneurial businesses for the past 10 years, most recently, as UK Managing Director at Innocent Drinks. Prior to Innocent, Jamie was Managing Partner and co-founder of Vesta Group, a venture capital company.

He is a Teaching Fellow in Entrepreneurship at London Business School, has an MBA from Harvard Business School and a BA from Oxford, and past jobs include number crunching at McKinsey and speech writing at the Confederation of British Industry.

In 2008, Jamie was named as a Young Global Leader by the World Economic Forum.

Since this column was published, Innocent Drinks has sold a share of the company to the Coca-Cola Company and Jamie has moved to Daylesford Organic as Chief Executive Officer.

More strength to your ARM

Financial Times, 3rd November 2007

Sir Robin Saxby was the founding Chief Executive
and Chairman of microprocessor technology company
ARM Holdings.

He explained to me that the hardest time for ARM was early on,
when the business went from about 30 to 60 people. Demand for
their products was booming — and much greater than the resources
— so they had to find a lot of people quickly, with the inevitable
requirement to train the new arrivals and at the same time deliver
to the customers.

His solution: you have to grit your teeth, hire professional
managers, and cope with the inevitable exit of a few disgruntled
members of staff. Robin hired Warren East, who is now Chief
Executive, from Texas Instruments. East put in a clear set of
processes and procedures.

It was the end of the old, 'fun' start-up and the birth of a proper
company. (I reckon that the precise moment when a company
goes from a tribe to a corporation is the day a lock appears on the
stationery cupboard.)

Seventeen years later, there are more than 1,700 people in ARM
and you can find their chip technology everywhere: if you have
anything small and digital, it will probably have an ARM product
inside. More advanced phones have two or three.

ARM developed a highly successful and scalable business model,
based not on shipping products but on delivering technology
through licensing and partnership. They design the digital engines,
which are licensed to semiconductor companies who then build
their own stuff around it.

Every client's chip is different, but they all use a standard ARM
building block. ARM has surreptitiously become the global standard in
embedded processors: ARM Partners shipped 2.5 billion chips last year.

124

If you are as successful as ARM you can of course give something back. Sir Robin has always had this approach: as a student at Liverpool University, he ran events, and bought every block in his hall of residence a washing machine and tumble dryer out of the profits. More recently he has helped set up a management school.

Sir Robin has always been good at spotting opportunities and talent. He started by fixing black and white TV sets for neighbours in the late 1950s. He noticed a particular trend in demand: people really wanted to watch the Queen's Christmas message and were also willing to pay good money for repairs during the festive period.

After working for Motorola, Henderson Security Systems and European Silicon Structures, he found himself in a pub with 12 engineers — the genesis of ARM. One of them, Tudor Brown, was appointed Head of Engineering. Today he is Chief Operating Officer. Two other engineers had a bit of a surprise: Jamie Urquhart and Mike Muller were told they were going to be in charge of sales and marketing respectively.

"The precise moment when a company goes from a tribe to a corporation is the day a lock appears on the stationery cupboard"

Sir Robin saw that Jamie was communicative and personable, a natural salesman, and that Mike had the essence of good marketing, the ability to describe what you have in clear ways that people can understand.

This is a key success factor for an ambitious start-up: getting the delivery people involved in sales and marketing. It is dangerous to have a 'silo mentality', where there is no communication between sales and delivery. ARM is clear proof that good engineers can sell. All you need is to be liked, able to listen and able to project. If customers like you, they might very well buy from you.

Today, Sir Robin has just finished his 1-year presidency of the Institution of Engineering and Technology, with a special focus

on inspiring schoolchildren to become engineers. He clearly
believes in fabricating well-rounded people and feels strongly
that engineers are quite capable of getting their heads around
marketing and even finance.

Sir Robin Saxby

*Sir Robin Saxby is
Chairman of Arolla
Partners Ltd. He was
founding CEO and
Chairman of ARM Holdings
plc, retiring in September
2007. He was Managing
Director of ES2 Ltd,
between 1986 and 1990 and CEO of Henderson
Security Systems from 1984 to 1986. His earlier
career was at Motorola Semiconductors and in
design and development with Rank Bush Murphy
and Pye TMC.*

*He is a Faraday medallist and Hon Fellow
of the IET where he served as President
from 2006 to 2007 and a Fellow of The Royal
Academy of Engineering. He has B Eng from
the University of Liverpool, where he is now
a visiting professor, Hon D Eng, University of
Liverpool, D Tech Loughborough and D U Essex.
He served as a Non-Executive Director of
Glotel plc and Sirius Communications.*

'Promises, Promises'

Financial Times, 29th March 2008

I always thought Keith Haviland had a bright future ahead of him.

Back in 1989, he was one of the shocked faces in the Slug and Lettuce when we announced that we had sold our company, The Instruction Set, to what would soon be part of Cap Gemini Ernst and Young. We had gone in an instant from 150 people on a mission to change the world to being a rather small part of the largest computer services company in Europe.

Some in the audience felt that the large company regime was not for them, and decided to start their own very successful start-ups. Keith decided he was happy within a big, structured organisation, but was soon headhunted to join Accenture.

His first project was working on a computer system for which he had no personal experience. He met that challenge and in a few years was made a partner. Today he runs a global network of delivery centres. He was therefore an obvious choice to find out what it means to deliver very large projects, something that the growing business has to become good at.

All businesses move from 'premise' to 'promise' fairly swiftly. They tell as many people as possible what they do and promise to do a good job for them. But how do you actually make these promises a reality? I asked Keith what were the keys for success.

It all starts, as you would expect, with people. Accenture hires the very best, and then provides a carefully designed induction programme to turn this raw material into people who really understand what the company is all about and what is expected of them, personally.

This is where fast-growing businesses can stumble in the early days. Everybody in the company offers to hire their friends and former colleagues. Logically this could grow exponentially, but in practice this method of recruitment tends to run out of steam after a while.

So recruitment companies are alerted, and you are soon faced with a large stack of candidates. The principals of the business want to read all the CVs and interview everybody, but this creates an enormous logjam. Keith says you must have a Human Resources Director to sort this out.

Then, it's all about getting things done. The Human Resources Director will arrange training for managers in leadership and for employees in teamwork. There will be the best project management tools that the business can afford. Everybody will have 6-monthly reviews where both managers and team members discuss, agree and later review objectives on both sides.

> "Hire the very best, and then turn this raw material into people who really understand the company and what is expected of them, personally"

When I pressed Keith for an example of a highly successful project, he described not a software development, but a campaign called 'Five Hundred in Five', where he set the objective of hiring 500 new people in 5 weeks for a new undertaking.

This was achieved ahead of time and proved highly motivational, thus mirroring the top two components of Maslow's famous 'Hierarchy of Needs': Self Actualisation (solving a difficult problem) and 'Esteem' (gaining the respect of others). This last element was reflected in his choice of reward: everyone on the project received a special t-shirt, as well as the usual benefits.

So his people knew that they had delivered successfully: they had been there, done that, and got the t-shirt.

Keith is now responsible for over 70,000 people — something to aspire to when your company passes its 30-person limit and you begin to think 'do we need more systems?'

Keith Haviland

Keith Haviland is the managing director of Accenture's Systems Integration (SI) business and the global Delivery Centre Network (DCN) for Technology.

On joining Accenture in 1990, Keith led large-scale complex technology programs for clients in a range of industries. Keith founded Accenture's first Delivery Centres in London in 1994 and in India in 2001 and then became the global lead for the network in 2002. It has now grown to over 40,000 people, with locations in North America, Latin America, Europe, Africa, India, the Philippines and China.

Since February 2009, Keith has also been responsible for Accenture's Systems Integration business which has over 30 years' deep SI experience serving more than 70 of the Global 100 organisations. The combined staff of SI and the Delivery Centres amount to approximately 70,000 people.

Keith has a degree in Mathematics and Management Science from Cambridge University and is the author of two books: UNIX Systems Programming and The Digital Lexicon.

www.accenture.com

Part Eight:

The R Word

When I started my *Financial Times* column, the world economy was booming; now it's a much different story...

I don't think there is a direct correlation between these two events! It has rather more to do with the banks, the regulators and a culture of quick returns with not enough questions asked.

In the end, however, life isn't about apportioning blame but getting on and fixing the mess. That's what entrepreneurs are best at, anyway.

While many of my more recent pieces mention the R-word, I have selected five with a specific recession theme to go in this section. I talk to entrepreneurship experts like Guy Rigby.

I look at the painful business of 'downsizing'; I go in search of some tips for anyone who has been 'downsized'; I look at the banks and try and point out a way forward for them. And I conclude on a positive note.

We are getting out of the recession; the people who are getting us out are not politicians or bankers, but entrepreneurs. They are hard at work sorting out the mess, right now.

Downsizing and After

Financial Times, 11th April 2009

There are plenty of companies emerging from the economic turmoil with full order books.

These lucky people are taking advantage of improved terms from their suppliers and the availability of good people. But many others are not, and even for the good ones, a recession is the time for some belt-tightening. The prudent Finance Director will have reviewed their company's costs and made savings without reducing the quality of their products and services.

But it is also common in hard times for there to be some redundancies. This can be a personal nightmare for an entrepreneur who started their company as a tribe, and then grew it into an organisation during the boom times.

Sadly, the case for losing certain people may be overwhelming, and may include some personal friends who were with them from the beginning. Such people can become de-motivated and gradually turn into 'psychic vampires', affecting everyone else in the organisation.

Of course, the case should not just be anecdotal but be the output of a formal review process where the individual's personal metrics for measuring success were mutually agreed in advance. Ideally, this should all be under the control of an HR specialist.

Once the sad but necessary work of downsizing has been done, careful thought must be given to the rest of the people in the company, the survivors. There will always be rumours circulating about further lay-offs despite the optimistic messages put out by management. Even though these are unfounded, good people may already be looking elsewhere for new opportunities.

My advice is to address these concerns head-on at a company event, but not as a formal presentation by the entrepreneur. A much better approach is to deliver difficult messages as part of an interview by an experienced external moderator, who must be allowed to ask the really hard questions, the ones that are on the audience's mind.

The entrepreneur must answer frankly and openly, but has the advantage of knowing the questions in advance. They can prepare accordingly, safe in the knowledge that, while the questions may be direct, the inquisitor will not ask any unplanned, awkward questions (unless they never want to moderate a conference again).

Once the bad news is out of the way and the unfounded rumours put firmly to bed, the next part of the day should be about the management's view on the best way forward; after all, they are the people responsible for future strategy and its implementation. Good leadership is all about having a vision for the future and clear communication of how this will be achieved.

> "Address these concerns head-on at a company event"

However, it is also important to be inclusive; the biggest complaints from unhappy staff are that no one listens to them and they feel they cannot make a difference. A third part of the day should give staff a chance to present their own ideas. People in a company are always closer to problems and customers than the management.

If given some encouragement, staff will always generate good ideas for improving the business, especially if you also give them the personal responsibility to implement their own ideas themselves. Not all ideas will work, but they should all be regarded as a useful learning experience.

Downsizing is a tough experience for everybody, but when done correctly it always makes the company stronger and better positioned for future opportunities. ▪

The Seven-Year Itch

Financial Times, 28th March 2009

Harry Freedman runs Career Energy, which helps people find new employment.

His business is the perfect bellwether of the careers market; when times are good, he is advising ambitious but bored people on radical career changes. In these hard times, much of his activity is in outplacement, helping often very dispirited people regain their self-esteem and find a new job.

Harry has written a very timely book, How to Find a Job in a Recession, which explains his process. He explains that looking for a job in a recession is different; the key is to be pro-active, and not just to wait for opportunities. You need to target the right opportunities and then present yourself in the right way.

Different people approach job-seeking very differently; introverts will spend ages perfecting their CV, filling it with relevant features, while others are extrovert and will rush off and network.

It is important to remember that both tasks need to be done; a brilliant CV which is not actively promoted will just gather dust, and a candidate with an outgoing personality but without the right collateral will be regarded as too much of a risk.

Harry works on both aspects, starting with where to look for potential jobs when nothing is being advertised. The key is in personal and on-line networking; there are many on-line tools to help raise your 'profile' (otherwise known as your 'personal brand'). Most of us now are on social networks, such as LinkedIn, which is specifically geared for job seekers.

> Raise your 'profile' (otherwise known as your 'personal brand')

Harry's book also covers the mechanics of responding to job advertisements, the best way to use recruitment consultants, how to make speculative approaches and the challenge of cold calling. Then it is all about the interview, an area where everyone, especially the most confident, needs coaching. An over-enthusiastic interviewee can talk themselves out of an opportunity in a few minutes.

Harry had some interesting views on life and a '7-year cycle' — something I have noticed with entrepreneurs, who often spend this amount of time on a project then move on.

He suggests that between 21 and 28, you should try as many things as possible.

From 28 to 35, you pick one of those things and make your first focused attempt at being successful.

Between 35 and 42, you might decide to try something different.

Between 42 and 49 you are often at the peak of your powers.

The years from 49 to 56 represent maturity, self-awareness and reflection.

Between 56 and 63 people start wondering about their legacy — will the world be a better place for them having been there?

From 63 onwards you should have the right combination of life skills and self-awareness to be an effective mentor.

Once you understand the mechanics of job-hunting and the cycles of life, you might eventually conclude that, in retrospect, a recession-driven, forced career move was the best thing that ever happened to you.

As Harry Freedman says in his book, there are still many great opportunities out there; all it requires is a positive mindset, and to understand both yourself and the job market.

Dr Harry Freedman

Dr Harry Freedman is Founder and Chief Executive of Career Energy, the UK's career advice consultancy. His varied career includes CEO roles in several SMEs and the voluntary sector. He has made many career changes, which is how he knows that nobody needs to work in a job to which they are not suited.

www.careerenergy.co.uk

How to Get a Job in a Recession by Harry Freedman is published by Infinite Ideas.

Banking on Success

Financial Times, 24th January 2009

The charm offensive from the high street banks
has already started.

Lloyds TSB has just launched its Charter for Small Businesses,
including passing on interest rate cuts and running some business
advice seminars. They promise that they would agree to any
reasonable request for short-term finance and do what they can
to support any viable business through temporary difficulties. The
other high street banks are making similar pronouncements.

I wonder if the banks realise that the attitude of many small
businesses has changed while they have been busy sorting
themselves out. To paraphrase Peter Finch in the film Network,
"We're as angry as hell and we're not going to take it anymore."

The current recession is not our fault; small businesses have not
been greedy, stupid and poorly self-regulated. We suddenly find
our credit squeezed and our customers' buying decisions delayed.
Our products and services are just as good; we find it very annoying
that it is now harder to sell and deliver them, through no fault of
our own.

But we entrepreneurs do not spend too long feeling sorry for
ourselves; we just get on with business, mindful that we are the
only ones who can save the economy. We are the people who
generate taxation revenue, not the ones that just spend it on what
we often regard as poorly executed initiatives.

We understand that 'boom and bust' is how the economy works.
The more sensible of us saved our cash during the boom times and
are now developing new business ideas during the recession when
opportunities abound for solving customer problems.

We have looked at the high street banks and have decided we
would like to deal with them in a new way. When they effectively
shut up shop to very early stage entrepreneurs, we moved to a

'cash and barter' economy. While interest rates are low, many entrepreneurs are bypassing the banks and storing their cash under the bed. No wonder the government printed more money; they are probably running out of bank notes.

Many established businesses that are being turned away by the banks are instead raising growth capital directly from angel investors. Bill Morrow runs Angels Den, an on-line portal connecting investors and entrepreneurs which also runs 'speed funding' events. He has 2,200 Angels registered and over 100 investments have already been made. Business is booming.

The banks will therefore face a much more difficult and competitive market when they return to the game. Entrepreneurs realise that all the high street banks are essentially identical with very similar services and interest rates; we remember with great clarity how loyal they were to us in this recession; we will shop around and go for the one that we like the most.

> "We have looked at the high street banks and have decided we would like to deal with them in a new way"

So the challenge for the banks is the same challenge as for us entrepreneurs; to be liked more than the competition. Their famous brands have been devalued by their own hands, so it is down to the individuals we meet in our local branches, how much we like them and feel that they understand our businesses.

The bank that will win the most new customers in this new competitive market will be the one that has invested money not just in advertising campaigns, but also in improving the interpersonal skills of their small business bank managers, especially in networking and customer service.

A good relationship works both ways, of course. The wise entrepreneur should either talk to the bank via a Finance Cornerstone or make sure they understand the basics of finance themselves. Banks have a right to expect this.

The days of the entrepreneur going cap in hand to the bank may be over. No more pleading for money to start their venture. Instead, how about this for an opening line: "Hello, I have been running a successful small business for a while and would like to deposit some money. How can you help me?"

Bill Morrow

Bill Morrow is founder and CEO of Angels Den, Europe's largest equity funding facilitators, who bring business Angels and entrepreneurs together.

www.angelsden.co.uk

Avoiding Failure
Financial Times, 21st March 2009

The recession is in full swing; recently, two of my friends' businesses have gone under, despite having healthy order books.

In both cases, the final coup de grace was delivered by their banks, which withdrew further credit. To a former salesperson, a company going into receivership despite having a good sales pipeline is a paradox, so for enlightenment I sought the advice of Guy Rigby, who heads up the entrepreneur group at accountants Smith & Williamson.

Guy points out that withdrawal of credit is a characteristic of a recession. Good economic conditions can paper over the cracks in weak businesses, but when credit becomes tight this no longer becomes possible. The key is to catch the real root causes of the business's problems before they become terminal.

For companies that are turning over more than £1 million, Smith & Williamson offer a free two-hour business 'Road Test'. They review 20 key areas of the business, highlight any where there are weaknesses and suggest solutions.

They first examine the strategy and business model; too often they find that companies are essentially pushing water uphill. They may be generating revenue from existing customers, but this may have declined over time, or even represent unprofitable business.

Failure to take necessary action in good time is the hallmark of weak or ineffective management. It may be time to refresh the talent at the top. While Smith & Williamson do not advocate changing entire management teams after a short series of poor results, they point out that complacency combined with an inability to act decisively under pressure are major factors in companies' failure.

The whole organisation may need to be reviewed if the company is over-staffed and poorly managed. But getting rid of underperforming or irrelevant people is not easy. It needs to be done fast: in the current climate people will be fearful for their jobs, and random discussion about this will reduce productivity even further. But it also needs to be done right: if the best-performing people think the axe is being wielded irrationally, they will start looking for a fairer employer.

Guy stresses that the challenges in a company are not just internal. Some of your customers may be difficult and unprofitable; their business terms should be re-negotiated or even politely terminated if no agreement can be found.

> "Failure to take necessary action in good time is the hallmark of weak or ineffective management"

This process can be unpleasant, especially if you have to say goodbye to some long-standing clients, but it is often cathartic. It is common for companies that go through this process to see a dip in turnover for the next year but to benefit from a significant increase in profits.

Another area of focus centres on the company's suppliers, who may have become unreliable or unprofitable. Again, this may involve people and companies you have dealt with for years and involve some personal embarrassment for the founders of the company, but your relationship with your suppliers should always be based on good business sense, not sentiment.

Sadly, the Smith & Williamson 'Road Test Your Business' offer came too late for my friends. My advice for them is to take a long holiday to repair and renew their relationship with their families, and then take President Obama's advice to "pick yourself up, dust yourself off and start all over again".

They should contact their immediate network of people, especially those with whom they have a high level of trust and respect, and identify a business opportunity that can generate cash quickly. With any luck they will soon be knocking on the doors of a bank again.

When they do, they might decide to look for a quite different type of bank. The incumbents in the banking market know they have to behave differently in the future, and some enterprising entrepreneurs I know are even thinking of starting their own. They are sure they can find customers, and they tell me that the mechanics of a bank that only takes deposits and makes loans are fairly straightforward.

Their only challenge is attracting the initial funding, so if you happen to have half a billion pounds lying about and want to help the UK's best cash-generating entrepreneurs, please let me know.

Guy Rigby

Guy Rigby is an experienced chartered accountant who has spent his career working with and around entrepreneurs. After qualifying, he joined Chrysalis, a well-known company in the music industry, prior to becoming Finance Director of British Fittings, a privately owned distribution group.

He was then responsible (as Managing Director and then Executive Chairman) for the development of a large international professional services network, and has been senior partner of a top-50 accounting firm. More recently, he implemented the development strategy for a well-known professional services group prior to its successful sale.

In 2007, Guy was joint-founder of the Non-Executive Directors Association (NEDA), formed to promote the benefits that non-executive directors bring to businesses of all sizes, whilst ensuring that they are properly trained and developed.

Guy joined Smith & Williamson in 2008 and leads the entrepreneurial services group.

www.smith.williamson.co.uk

Business as Usual

Financial Times, 31st Jan 2009

The last week in January is traditionally the most depressing of the year.

Post-Christmas euphoria has vanished and the realities of the New Year sink in. This year, these realities have been particularly gloomy, with the long-awaited announcement by the government that the recession has officially arrived. However, there's still work to be done: for entrepreneurs, it's 'business as usual'.

> "If anyone has any lingering doubts about the long-term future of UK PLC then they should spend some time with this collection of bright-eyed 16 to 19-year-olds"

For me, this means speaking to business people. My first 'gig' of the week was a series of small-business events organised by South Oxfordshire District Council and the Birmingham Business Club. I delivered a positive message, calling my presentation 'Preparing for The Next Upturn', and the mood of the audiences matched my optimism.

Everyone felt that they had successful businesses delivering real value to customers who still had both needs and money. Some buying decisions were being delayed, but generally the long-term prospects were good, as long as your business was well-managed and not saddled with debt.

There was some discussion about the global economy: we agreed that the problems originated in the USA and that the solution would come from there as well. President Obama will have to stimulate his economy and will create new confidence, which will inevitably trickle down to the UK. In the meantime, we had businesses to run.

My next engagement was to address the sales force of a major IT services supplier. They, too, seemed relatively untroubled by

this is how **yoodoo** it.

the economic threat, as they had long-term contracts (many with central or local government) and, crucially, experience from the last recession. Actually, they were being inundated with job applications and were enjoying hiring the very best people, especially from their less well-managed competitors.

This reminded me that, whatever your opinion on the percentage of our GDP directly controlled by government, this sector will always be a good source of work.

My final engagement of the week was at the National Enterprise Academy (NEA), founded by entrepreneur, Tycoon and Dragon's Den panellist Peter Jones.

The NEA offers young people the first-ever full-time programme in enterprise and entrepreneurship. If anyone has any lingering doubts about the long-term future of entrepreneurship in general and UK PLC in particular, then they should spend some time with this collection of bright-eyed 16 to 19-year-olds.

Peter Jones CBE

Peter Jones CBE founded Phones International Group in 1998 and now has interests in a wide range of companies, inlcuding publishing, new media, television, entertainment, food products, the environment and product design. He founded the NEA in 2009.

The NEA has facilities in Amersham, Manchester and Sheffield:

http://www.thenea.org.uk

Many of these were already in business. They all had great business ideas, including property development, computer hardware and consultancy. One had run a successful club night.

The most enjoyable part of the event was hearing about how they were all determined to make a difference once they had achieved some success.

This would start by giving their families the financial security (and even work opportunities) currently denied to them; then they would start solving the social and economic problems of the world.

One of them asked me for some contacts in hedge funds. I explained that my network was not very good in this area, plus I had a sneaking suspicion that these people were partly responsible for our current malaise. We agreed that what was needed was a new-generation source of funding, tailored for entrepreneurs who want to make a real difference in the world.

So I end the last week in January 2009 in a mood of neither gloom nor panic, but quiet confidence. For those entrepreneurs who have good management skills and a positive mindset, it is 'business as usual'. ▨

Part Nine:

Success Stories

Enough recession, already!

Probably the nicest thing about writing my *Financial Times* column is that I get to meet some great entrepreneurs, people who have really followed their vision and made a difference. They all have great stories to tell.

So without further ado...

Quite Interesting

Financial Times, 8th December 2007

You're probably familiar with QI, the TV quiz show fronted by Stephen Fry.

The QI books are its physical manifestation, a potpourri of fascinating information and excellent jokes, expertly crafted under the direction of comedy legend John Lloyd, whose previous credits include Spitting Image and Blackadder. Easy for him, then, you might think, but look a little closer and you will find a story of genuine struggle and entrepreneurship, and a surprisingly subversive agenda.

At the end of the 80s, with two lifetime achievement awards under his belt, John retired from broadcasting and threw himself into the corporate world, directing dozens of comedy adverts, most famously for Barclaycard with Rowan Atkinson's bumbling spy.

Jetting around the world, an acknowledged master of both television comedy and its commercial offshoot, John had a sudden realisation. Despite a passion for knowledge that had been with him since boyhood, he really didn't know anything... Science does amazing things, but nobody actually knows what gravity, laughter, viruses, consciousness or even life itself actually are.

Back home in the village pub, he outlined these thoughts to his neighbour John Mitchinson, a senior publisher on gardening leave. They agreed that a new approach to learning was needed. Rather than peddle false certainty, they would admit ignorance and help people find their own ways to knowledge by stimulating interest in the world.

Part of this subversion would be the debunking of conventional wisdom, another part the dissemination of quirky facts. Did you know that female kangaroos have three vaginas, that the steam engine was invented in ancient Greece or that only one species of frog in the world goes 'ribbit'?

So, from a tiny serviced office in Oxford, with two recent graduates as researchers, the two Johns set out to change the people's perception of the universe. Given John Lloyd's contact list, the TV series was the easiest way to begin, so they wisely took that route. But how to follow that? They decided that QI needed a physical expression, too, and decided to start a private members' club.

Raising some £750,000 in private investment, they opened the QI Club in Oxford, meticulously furnishing it with an excellent restaurant, a welcoming café-bar, an eclectic bookshop that only sold 'quite interesting' books, and a terrific programme of events.

"Rather than peddle false certainty, they would admit ignorance and help people find their own ways to knowledge by stimulating interest in the world"

It was a big mistake. The mechanics of running a catering business are not for amateurs, however gifted; the pressures of staff and financial management are intense, and, from the very start they began to lose money.

After 3 years, working all hours and sinking all of their savings into the project, they concluded that the club required significant extra capitalisation, beyond the means of themselves or the will of their investors. They arranged a trade sale of the club, and refocused their efforts into their core businesses: television and books.

They have not looked back. The television show attracts over five million viewers. They currently have three books in the Amazon top 40 and a bestseller in the New York Times' list. The first book has appeared in 23 other countries from China to Brazil. QI's plan — to amuse, inform and educate the world by stealth — is clearly working.

A core belief of QI is that anything can be made interesting if looked at long enough, closely enough or in the right way. They recently applied this theory to the first QI corporate video, for a multinational insurance company.

The Finance Director had just been elevated to the top job, and wanted to get across that a backroom number cruncher can also have the vision and personal qualities to lead a global company.

John filmed him talking with five professors from INSEAD, the business school headquartered in France — gaining insights into subjects as diverse as IT, climate change and corporate responsibility. The new CEO, never before known to take off his tie, turned out to be a natural on camera: warm and open-minded with a quick sense of humour. And, of course, it was all quite interesting.

A pub lunch with John left me buzzing with optimism. His almost throwaway comment "you should do entrepreneurship for kids" has had me thinking of little else since. When I speak in schools and universities about starting businesses, they really seem to get it.

My biggest challenge is to explain that not all bosses are like Alan Sugar and that entrepreneurship doesn't necessarily have to involve facing a panel of 'Dragons'.

For me, the lessons of QI are clear: start with a great idea, stick to what you know, stick at it, but have the courage to cut your losses if you must.

Meanwhile, I'm off to get the splendidly titled QI interactive DVD game 'Strictly Come Duncing' for my 10-year-old son for Christmas. If he's more engaged by the mixture of meticulously researched facts and really good jokes than destroying intergalactic alien monsters, then that will be Very Interesting...

John Lloyd

After a promising start at King's School, Canterbury, John Lloyd went to a pub near Trinity College, Cambridge where he was eventually head-hunted by a man in a beard from the BBC. He started The News Quiz, 'Quote... Unquote', The News Huddlines and To The Manor Born.

He produced Not The Nine O'Clock News, Spitting Image and Blackadder and played a key role in The Hitchhiker's Guide To The Galaxy and Mr Bean. In his spare time he shot TV commercials.

In 2002 he set up Quite Interesting Limited with John Mitchinson. The panel show QI first aired on BBC2 in September 2003 with Lloyd producing and Mitchinson masterminding the research and writing. In 2008 it won the Royal Television Society Award for Best Entertainment Programme and the British Comedy Award for Best Comedy Panel Show.

John Mitchinson

John Mitchinson has worked in the book trade for more than 20 years. He was the original Marketing Director of Waterstone's, leaving in 1995 to become Managing Director first of the newly independent Harvill Press and then Cassell & Co.

He published a diverse list of authors and subjects including The Beatles, Michael Palin and Brewer's Dictionary of Phrase and Fable. John is also a Vice President of the Hay Festival, chairs the London International Centre for Storytelling and is a fellow of the RSA. In his spare time he keeps rare breed pigs.

Real Eating

Financial Times, 15th December 2007

Many top people have the same dream: to quit their high-powered job and open up a smart restaurant.

What better way to combine a passion for good food with well-honed business skills?

Helena Hudson has done just that. She spent many years in a media-buying agency. When it was sold she saw this as a perfect opportunity to open a restaurant in her hometown, Brighton, which also featured a delicatessen and bakery (she had seen places like this in London).

This is a common pattern. Sahar Hashemi wondered why she could not get a New York-style skinny latte in London and Coffee Republic was born. Simon Woodroffe saw conveyor-belt sushi in Tokyo and brought it to London, founding Yo! Sushi.

> "Eventually 'gut feel', the prime driver for most successful entrepreneurs, took over"

Helena had always been passionate about good food; her favourite bedtime reading material was Cordon Bleu cookbooks. She combined this with her business skills, first undertaking meticulous research into potential properties, then likely footfall and the competitive landscape in Brighton — anything she could study and analyse.

Eventually 'gut feel', the prime driver for most successful entrepreneurs, took over; she walked into a former art gallery in Hove, and knew at once exactly where everything was going to go. The Real Eating Company was born.

The best thing about starting your own business is that you can choose the right job for yourself. Helena decided she would be best running the operation, not working in the kitchen, running the floor or serving in the delicatessen.

The first hire was crucial: the Head Chef. Next, she sensibly found a bookkeeper (most early start-ups fail due to cash-flow problems), and then a General Manager to run all of the day-to- day operations.

But it was not all plain sailing; the Head Chef left after 18 months, and she has had several General Managers in their 4 years of operation. Helena explained that the restaurant business is characterised by significant 'churn' in staff, a pattern I have seen in many other customer-facing businesses.

This must be very difficult and time-consuming for the early-stage restaurant entrepreneur. In our Beermat entrepreneurship model we talk about the need for 'cornerstones', people who are vital to the business and who probably should have a significant share in the business.

This is not always feasible in the restaurant business unless the chef themselves is the entrepreneur, like Gordon Ramsay or Jamie Oliver. In Helena's case, she has to find the right person with appropriate skills and persuade them to cook in the style which she feels is right for the Real Eating Company. She then expects that in 18 months or so they may want to leave and start their own restaurant.

Helena Hudson

Helena Hudson spent 16 years in marketing and media communications working with blue-chip clients at major advertising and media agencies, the last 8 years as a board director, managing a company with a turnover of over £75million, with a staff of 95.

During her career, Helena's clients have been varied and include Ford Motor Co, Argos, Golden Wonder, L'Oreal, MGM Home Entertainment, Somerfield Supermarkets, Elizabeth Arden, BUPA, Toys R Us and the Central Office of Information.

She now owns and runs the Real Eating Company.

www.real-eating.co.uk

The rest of the staff pose an even bigger problem. They tend to be young, ambitious and personable, but they have the terrible power to destroy your brand in an instant by falling out with a customer.

All this means that the restaurant entrepreneur probably has to spend as much time using their people skills in attracting, training and retaining their staff, as in the intricacies of the business operation.

It seems that everyone learns how to do this the hard way, a step at a time, learning from their mistakes. Helena has done this and successfully moved to the next stage, scaling the business.

When I worked in the telecommunications industry, we often spoke about Metcalfe's Law, which states that the value of a network is proportional to the square of the number of the users in the system. The same proportionality unfortunately applies to the amount of hassle in a person-based organisation.

Still, Helena Hudson appears to have what it takes to meet this challenge. So far she has opened restaurants in Hove and Lewes and cafes in Horsham, Bournemouth and Brighton.

Carpe Diem

Financial Times, Saturday 19th January 2008

I'm sure many of you will recognise the quote 'Carpe Diem'.

It was popularised in the film Dead Poets Society, where the inspirational teacher played by Robin Williams encourages his pupils to abandon conformity, 'seize the day' and fulfil their promise.

It is the perfect motto for the aspiring entrepreneur. What differentiates an entrepreneur from a normal person is their ability to spot a business opportunity and — this is the real crunch — to then actually go out and do something about it. Seize the day; don't just sit around saying how nice it is.

Judy Naaké is a perfect example. Her father was an entrepreneur, so perhaps it was in her genes. However, her early working life was unremarkable; she sold jewellery and then was part of the promotions team for a cigarette company, although she never smoked herself. Later she ran a health club and worked front of house for her father's restaurant.

This was not fulfilling enough, so during the day she became a sales agent for a skin care product. One day she came across St Tropez, an American tanning product, which had been turned down by everyone else. But Judy was convinced this product was a winner.

There had been other tanning products before, but all were difficult to apply and left streaks; this one avoided these twin pains (it was also well priced and had excellent packaging). Her only concern was that beauty salons might have worries about how to apply the product correctly.

Her brilliant idea was to offer self-tanning workshops for £25 on Sundays and Mondays, turning her product idea into a service. If nobody signed up, she would not run the workshops. To keep costs down, she made the delegates' sandwiches herself the night before. Soon she was running them the length and breadth of the country.

The rest, as they say, is history. When she finally sold out the company was turning over upwards of £16 million.

I am sure Judy never anticipated that her business would develop from a £12,000 bank loan to a multi-million dollar business. Like most entrepreneurs, I expect she did little formal market research or bothered to spend hundreds of hours poring over spreadsheets; she just put some product in the boot of her car and got on with it.

Of course, she had the successful combination of being in the right place at the right time, and knowing how to make the best of that opportunity.

Celebrities flocked to her door; Judy has a dream client list which includes Victoria Beckham, Cat Deeley, Hermione Norris and Elle McPherson. This resulted in fantastic PR, which Judy regards as a significant driver for her success.

With a successful product business comes the need to develop indirect channels. For example, in the software industry there are dealers, distributors, resellers, value added resellers and master distributors. Judy now has an extensive retail network in Selfridges and Debenhams, as well as the traditional beauty salons.

> "Like most entrepreneurs, she did little formal market research; she just put some product in the boot of her car and got on with it"

The danger is that indirect channels can distance the entrepreneur from their customers, and I always advise start-ups to cherish a few early accounts and to continue to deal with them directly, however large you grow.

They gave you a chance when you were relatively unknown, so the least you should do is always return their phone calls personally. But they can also be your eyes and ears in the market, alerting you to competitors, especially those with innovative products.

But more importantly, they can act as your evangelists and might even become 'mavens', a Yiddish term popularised by

Malcolm Gladwell in The Tipping Point. Mavens are people who have disproportionate influence on other members of their network.

Judy still deals with the A-List clients personally. Even if they are not able to provide a celebrity endorsement, they will certainly attract other pop stars, television presenters, actors and supermodels to St Tropez Tan.

So entrepreneurship, as aptly demonstrated by Judy Naaké, can be neatly summarised as 'find an opportunity', 'harvest the day' and 'always provide excellent personal service to the key influencers in your market'.

If you are a big success, you might even leave a legacy and be remembered in the history books. I would rather be remembered as a successful entrepreneur than a Dead Poet. █

Judy Naaké

Judy Naaké is best known for bringing the St Tropez self-tanning range to the UK and building the brand into the market leader within the UK through a combination of strong sales, marketing and PR.

Judy began in the humble surroundings of her father's fruit shop, but even then showed signs of future success by demonstrating a keenness to sell! Following a hugely successful career in promotions, primarily with John Player Special, she moved into the beauty industry; the sector where she was eventually to make her name and leave her mark.

Key to the success of Decleor, Darphin and the hugely popular Australian Bodycare Tea Tree range, she expanded her business taking on the European distributorship for the then-unknown St Tropez. Several thousand tans later, she is widely recognised as one of the most successful entrepreneurs in the country.

www.st-tropez.com

'A Place of Your Own'

Financial Times, 26th April 2008

It is a common entrepreneurial dream to create a special place.

This could be a shop, a restaurant, an art gallery, where everyone can enjoy themselves and spend money, especially with their friends and other people they like.

I get this pitched to me almost on a daily basis. A budding entrepreneur has spotted a gap in the market. They are definitely going to address this; all they need is the right property. As soon as this happens, everything will fall into place and people will flock in.

Alas, if only this were true. Finding the right property but in the wrong location can lead to misery and then bankruptcy. I explain that I have a better model, which involves the aspiring entrepreneur test-driving their idea before they get their premises.

First, they need to understand their market; are there other people like themselves, dissatisfied with the way things are done now, and, more importantly, actually willing to pay for something better?

"Retail magic: a genuine empathy for people and a visible delight in service"

If there are, then they should try out a service model, perhaps first delivering their delicious fairtrade food to busy people in their offices. If you are good at what you do, they will tell their friends. Eventually you will hit a 'tipping point': when you have developed a big enough client base, you will be able to attract a proportion of them to your premises.

A perfect example of someone who took this approach is Emma Willis, the only female shirt- maker in Jermyn Street. She started, almost by accident, selling Turnbull and Asser shirts to City boys at their desks. She was very good at this, a combination of charm, glamour, and a willingness to deal with the inevitable power haircuts, loud ties and rampant egos back in the 80s.

this is how **yoodoo** it.

Then she discovered something surprising. She was actually really interested in the manufacturing of the shirts. And what was more, she reckoned she could do a better job (a classic entrepreneur motivation).

She became involved in everything: the fabrics, the design, the cutting and the stitching, and ended up buying a South London shirt factory, to secure English manufacturing for all her shirts.

She bought luxurious cottons from Switzerland, and had her own silk woven in Italy, combining the strong English style of make with soft European fabrics, evolving her own individual look, described early on by Vogue as 'inimitable English style', at a time when Jermyn Street was simply imitating itself.

Then it was time to set up her own shop. She already had a loyal customer base, the respect of her suppliers and of her competition. A happy customer was willing to become an investor, and Emma Willis Shirts opened on Jermyn Street.

Emma Willis

Emma Willis opened her Jermyn Street men's shop in 2000, selling shirts ties, pyjamas, dressing gowns, boxer shorts, cashmere and socks. All her product is made in England, using the most luxurious Swiss and Sea Island cottons and Italian silks.

Her style has been described by British Vogue as 'inimitable English style'. Emma Willis shirts are also available in Saks 5th Avenue in the United States, Selfridges in London and Le Globe in Tokyo.

www.emmawillis.com

Then Emma discovered something else about herself, a trait I refer to as 'retail magic'. Everyone serving the public in a shop, restaurant or other public-facing establishment should be polite, helpful and professional. But some also have an extra quality, a genuine empathy for people and a visible delight in service, often characterised by an ability to remember people's names as well as their buying habits.

She told me that she can spot the characteristics of a customer as they walk through the door: the casual browser or the serious enthusiast; the ones who want to discuss every detail of the shirt or the ones who want to be left alone; and most importantly, the ones who will spend money.

I sensed that Emma's biggest source of pride is the beautifully appointed shop in a very famous street with her own name over the door; a real sense of achievement and belonging, a place of her own.

Perfect Timing

Financial Times, 31st May 2008

Successful entrepreneurs seem to have an in-built sense of timing.

Nobody illustrates this more perfectly than Brent Hoberman, co-founder of lastminute.com.

He came from an entrepreneurial family, so despite a traditional education and early jobs in management consultancies, he was always looking for that big opportunity. He first thought of lastminute.com many years before its launch, but realised the time was not right and that he lacked the necessary experience.

Learning his trade at internet service provider LineOne and then at internet auction start-up QXL, he finally managed to persuade former co-worker Martha Lane Fox that his idea had some value. They complemented each other nicely; he had the basic idea and an understanding of the necessary technology, she was very well organised and a good people person.

> "They ignored the naysayers and got on with building the business"

Lastminute.com was based on a simple human need, the desire to do something at the last moment. But it attracted plenty of scepticism, especially from former colleagues, who could find plenty of very sensible reasons why it was not going to work: too new, too radical, and too difficult.

Brent and Martha did what all entrepreneurs do; they ignored the naysayers and got on with building the business. The timing was, of course, perfect. In the dotcom euphoria of 1999-2000, they found themselves able to float their company only 18 months after launch. During the roadshow their valuation went up 67%, and they arrived on the stock market on the exact day that NASDAQ hit its peak, in March 2000.

We all now scoff at the madness of the dotcom bubble, but lastminute.com was a proper business: it grew steadily and profitably before being sold in May 2005 to Sabre Holdings, owner of the Travelocity online travel business.

Brent stayed there for a couple more years, but is now working on a number of new ventures, notably home furniture site mydeco, where he now spends 4 days a week as Executive Chairman. This idea was based on the pain he went through trying to decorate his own house, even though his wife is an experienced interior designer.

The idea passed a few simple sanity checks, for example checking that nobody else was already doing the same thing and speaking to as many people in the industry as possible to see if they also thought it a good idea. But Brent still works on the 'ignorance is bliss' method; if you know too much about the potential pitfalls, then you will soon talk yourself out of it.

Brent is lucky: he has significant leverage with people he has made rich in the past, who will be willing to invest significant sums of money in an essentially unproven idea. These people are buying into a dream, but they do so on the basis that Brent not only has business experience and a good team, but also that most essential of entrepreneurial traits, timing.

Brent Hoberman

Brent Hoberman co-founded lastminute.com in April 1998 with Martha Lane Fox and was CEO and took the company to profit and gross bookings of over $2bn.

The company floated in March 2000 when the dot-com bubble was at its peak — the IPO Board Director of Guardian Media Group. From January, 2007 he took on the role of Non-Executive Chairman of Wayn.com — a travel and leisure social network with over 13 million members. Brent is also an angel investor in several internet companies including Viagogo, Wayn.com and moveme.com.

Giving Back

Financial Times, 28th June 2008

It is common for successful entrepreneurs, once they
have made a successful exit from their businesses, to
support charities and mentor young people.

Alex van Someren found an even more interesting way of 'giving back'.

Alex's career started when he was 14 and wrote off to the local
computer company Acorn saying how much he liked their product.
They sent back an encouraging reply, but probably didn't expect
him to turn up on their doorstep on the first day of his holidays.

Hermann Hauser gave him a computer to play with, and Alex
returned the next day with a cassette tape of a Star Trek game
ported from a Commodore 64. No work was done at Acorn that day
while everyone played the game, and his future career path was set.

His father probably had different plans for him; a successful
entrepreneur with his own line of biofeedback machines, he sent
his son to Eton. But despite mixing with the likes of David Cameron
and Boris Johnson, the young van Someren decided that university
or even A-Levels were not for him. Instead, he secured a job at
Acorn, working on the BBC Micro for a couple of years.

He then realised that there were plenty of development projects
for good programmers. He designed the first electronic version of
the Autocue, and later realised that there was a relatively simple
way to speed up the chip in the Acorn computer for a relatively
modest £99. Subsequent projects included an Ethernet networking
card and a way of putting an Intel chip in the Acorn computer,
allowing it to run PC applications.

In each case his business model was very straightforward: find
a successful product and develop a simple way of enhancing it
before the manufacturer worked out how to do it themselves. This
required fast prototyping, simple manufacture and well-developed
channels to sell the products directly to the end-users.

It also required the understanding that this was a 2-year window of opportunity, and the most important tasks were to hire the right management and to bow out gracefully at the right time, moving on to the next idea. In between ventures, Alex also looked for service revenue, such as training, to tide him over the lean times.

This model served him very well, and he eventually found what turned out to be 'the big one'. With the rise of the internet came the rise of e-commerce. But many people were concerned about the security issues of online payment. Your credit card details had to be encrypted at your end, and decrypted at the other end.

We are all now used to seeing a little padlock appear at the bottom of our web browser, but data encryption requires significant processing at the supplier end so that people do not get stuck in a queue, lose interest and depart before the transaction is complete.

> "Find a successful product and develop a simple way of enhancing it before the manufacturer worked out how to do it themselves"

Alex developed a neat and cheap solution to this pain, and then found a first customer, a share-trading company keen to avoid buying dozens of expensive servers. In 2000, his company nCipher floated successfully on the London Stock Exchange.

Alex handed over to the management last year. He is now giving back, regularly shaking down his high net worth chums for The Prince's Trust and providing mentoring as Entrepreneur in Residence at the Judge Business School in Cambridge.

He also managed to 'give something back' in a more unconventional way. nCipher raised £100 million and spent a proportion of that on interesting acquisitions and on developing the company. But they eventually decided that spending the rest of the money, around £65 million, just for the sake of it was unnecessary and wasteful, so they gave it back to the investors.

this is how **yoodoo** it.

While social enterprise and corporate social responsibility
are all the rage nowadays, you could follow Alex van Someren's
example and spare a thought for an especially worthy group:
your shareholders.

Alex van Someren

*Alex van Someren grew up
near Cambridge, became
involved with local firm
Acorn Computers as a young
teenager, leaving school
at 17 to join the company.
In 1996 he co-founded
nCipher, with venture
capital backing, to develop internet security
products using cryptography.*

*nCipher plc was listed on the London
Stock Exchange in 2000 and was
subsequently sold to Thales SA in 2008.
After woprking as a Dealmaker for the UK
Trade and Investment Global Entrepreneur
Programme, he has recently joined Amadeus
Capital as a Partner.*

*He still lives in Cambridge with his wife and
three children, where he is an active member
of the local entrepreneurial community.*

Eager to Please

Financial Times, 5th July 2008

Kristin Syltevik is founder and CEO of Hotwire, which specialises in PR for high-technology companies.

All around the UK you can hear the sound of belts tightening and budgets being cut. Those of us that have been around for a while know that this is just the natural way of things. We may indeed be moving into recession, or 'winter', but 'spring' is just around the corner, and we should prepare accordingly.

Many companies are feeling the pinch. The first to suffer are always the service providers as customers look carefully at any discretionary spending, such as training. This is, of course, a false economy. When times are tough you should spend more on training your people, especially in sales and customer service. The best way to get out of a recession is always to sell more.

This is difficult for some, especially those that do not regard themselves as natural salespeople; I spend a good amount of my time teaching sales to the professional classes: consultants, lawyers, accountants, engineers and bank managers.

Their challenge is that, on paper, their organisations are identical to their competitors; they have a set of expert skills and some great customers. But how can they differentiate their companies, and in a tough economic climate show that they provide an excellent return on investment?

One of the most competitive service industries is public relations. There are hundreds of companies out there, all theoretically providing the same set of services. Only the smartest will survive the upcoming recession, and many are suffering, as customers delay their spending or use in-house resources.

Kristin Syltevik is founder and CEO of Hotwire, who specialise in PR for high-technology companies and have a cabinet full of awards to prove their credentials. She explained that from the

this is how **yoodoo** it.

early days they focused on several key areas to succeed in a highly challenging and competitive market.

The natural approach of a PR company is always to stress their creativity, which is very effective when selling in the boom times. During a recession, much better sales slogans are: 'value for money', 'effective use of budget', and 'detailed analysis of costs'.

Syltevik explained that the most important aspect of service provision is measurement; how can you prove that you are providing value for money with your services? She approached a professor of PR at a university and together they designed a bespoke set of tools to constantly test the effectiveness of what they were doing for their clients, to demonstrate that they were providing value for money at all times.

She explained the next most important aspect is having detailed industry knowledge. The people in her company need to know as much about their specialist industries as their customers. This requires significant research and then making the right information available to the customer exactly when they need it, in the form of industry analysis, press coverage, white papers and interviews with industry figures and analysts.

"The best way to get out of a recession is always to sell more"

Another of Hotwire's important differentiators is their pan-European coverage, with offices in London, Madrid, Paris, Frankfurt and Milan, so they attract pan-European companies with significant PR budgets.

This can be difficult for small organisations, but many companies have technical people on-site at customer locations. They should always ask the client if they can let them have some dedicated office space which can become a sales focus for other departments in the same client and even new business in the local area. This should be for a suitable consideration, of course; perhaps some free consultant days on that new project they were considering.

Syltevik's final recommendation for success in a tough market was to hire only the best people. The main differentiator for service companies is the quality of their staff, which should be emphasised in all product literature and on the web site.

The downside of this is that inevitably some of your 'stars' will one day leave and form their own companies, but Syltevik was philosophical about this, explaining that this was the way of things, to be expected if you hire the best people and she always lets these people leave with good grace; there is space in the market for everybody.

But if there was just one particular personal attribute she looks for when hiring people it is 'eager'. In PR, as in all other service industries, you should be eager to please, eager to listen and eager to prove your value.

The last two attributes are particularly important now when times are tight, but soon the new shoots will be coming through, and it will once more be the right season to be creative.

Kristin Syltevik

Kristin Syltevik is MD of Hotwire, an award-winning PR agency which she co-founded in 2000. Hotwire has offices in London, Boston, Frankfurt, Paris, Madrid and Milan, as well as two sister agencies, Skywrite Communications and 33 Digital.

www.hotwirepr.com

Animal Magic

Financial Times, 4th April 2009

Many people are now starting web-based businesses
which are completely virtual.

They have no formal offices or even full-time staff. But there will
always be a need for local services, which require fixed premises,
such as restaurants, shops and bars.

Success in this field is difficult. First, there is the issue of
location: you can be just one street away from that most highly
desired commodity — 'passing trade' — and remain empty. Get that
right, and you still have to out-execute the competition, which
may already be operating a very similar establishment within
walking distance. Finally, if you are successful you will want to
replicate your model and scale your business, which brings a whole
new set of problems.

Someone who recognised these challenges and successfully met
them is Brendan Robinson, founder of the Village Vet. He arrived
in the UK as a fresh-faced graduate of a top veterinary college in
his native South Africa, and learnt his trade at the PDSA, the UK's
leading animal charity.

Brendan loved this experience, and reckons he did more animal
surgery in his 18 months there than most vets do in a lifetime. He
then found a suitable practice in Hampstead run by a vet who had
one eye on his impending retirement. He became a partner, and
soon bought out his colleague.

Brendan set about making the practice somewhere the local
residents would feel comfortable in bringing their pets, so he
furnished the place in the style of the homes in the area, with
plenty of stripped pine and natural light. Then he removed the
rather forbidding medical uniforms, replacing white coats with
casual wear, and greeted all the customers and their pets with a
friendly smile.

He puts his success down to being genuinely passionate about people and animals. People picked up this natural empathy; business was booming and he was soon looking for a second premises.

A second location is always an important milestone for any premises-based business; recording artists also talk about the 'difficult second album'. Brendan sensibly found empty premises less than a mile away in Highgate, which was actually nearer for many of his customers, who were happy to switch.

Once the right systems are in place, the challenge is always finding people who are able and willing to deliver the proven formula. They must have the right technical qualifications and expertise, but just as important are the people skills; subject matter experts can often appear intimidating to customers. Scolding a customer for not bringing in their pet earlier is not the right way to treat a person already deeply distressed by their animal's condition and suffering.

> "A second location is always an important milestone for any premises-based business"

Brendan learned the hard way how to knock the rough edges off brilliant vets who lacked the right social and customer service skills. He achieved this through external training, backed up by regular internal discussions about best practice and shared experiences.

As well as expanding a simple but clear model, Brendan is a keen innovator. His ideas include installing a hydrotherapy pool for animals recovering from surgery and flying in an animal cardiologist from Belgium once a month.

The Village Vet is now a very successful chain with 16 practices in London and Cambridge, and 24-hour hospitals in each location. Regular customers benefit from a Pet Privilege loyalty scheme and they are about to launch their own pet insurance scheme.

Brendan Robinson is an advocate of small, local medical care, and thinks this approach would work well for the NHS as an alternative to big, centralised hospitals which try to be all things to all people. Virgin Healthcare will soon be launched to do exactly this; they would do well to model the success of the Village Vet.

Brendan Robinson

Brendan Robinson was born in Cape Town and qualified as a vet in Onderstepoort in South Africa. He arrived in the UK in January 1984 and purchased Belsize Park Vet Surgery on 1st October 1989. He built up a veterinary group of 16 practices and two 24-hour hospitals over the next 20 years, setting up six surgeries and purchasing nine others.

www.villagevet.co.uk

Part Ten:

Social Entrepreneurship

Many of the young people who come to me for help are, in one of two senses, social entrepreneurs.

Some are busy trying to save the planet or help disadvantaged people directly. Others want to make money, but to do so ethically and have plans on how to combine that with doing some good in the world.

Such encounters give me great hope for the future; the blame for our current misfortune lies with the greedy, arrogant and stupid, not 'capitalism' in some general sense.

Capitalism is highly flexible — these young people plan to put it to a lot better use than some of their elders have managed to.

'Give While You Live'

Financial Times, 19th April 2008

Over a century ago Sir Titus Salt built the village of Saltaire to provide self-contained living space for the workers at his cotton mills.

This is the traditional model of philanthropy: make money and then give it to causes you deem worthy. Today's social entrepreneurs show a newer approach to 'good business'.

Social entrepreneurship is a topic that comes up a lot when I speak to young people. There is a definite a change in the zeitgeist, a natural swing from the 'greed is good' mentality of the 80s. In the 60s, the idealist took to the streets and espoused left-wing politics; today he or she is much more practical.

> "A social enterprise has to be run in exactly the same way as any other business"

One such person is Craig Dearden-Phillips MBE, who has written a book about his experiences, called Your Chance to Change the World: The No-fibbing guide to Social Entrepreneurship. He is the founder of Speaking Up, an organisation that makes sure that people who have no say in their lives, because of their learning difficulties or mental ill health, get heard and involved, especially in finding useful employment.

Craig started his career in the social care sector but found the system, in his own words, "a very expensive way to destroy people's lives". Like many an entrepreneur before him, he decided to start his own organisation and do it better. He faced the common challenge of the new start-up: creating enough credibility to start generating revenue, in his case from local authorities and other government sources.

Craig relied on help and support from his mentors and found the right 'cornerstones' for his business, but still made a few mistakes

this is how **yoodoo** it.

along the way, inevitable when you are essentially making it up as you go along, the standard path of the first-time entrepreneur.

But he now has a highly successful enterprise with over 100 people, and has opened up offices around the country. This involved him in winning competitive tenders from local authorities (ask any small business how tough this is). An added complication is that success for him means taking on people as staff who used to be on the books as clients.

It is clear when speaking with Craig that a social enterprise has to be run in exactly the same way as any other business: "This is not the fluffy world that a lot of FT readers will imagine — it's about taking a serious, business-like approach to urgent social issues."

He reminds me of his obligation to turn a profit every quarter and of his cast-iron insistence on recruiting and retaining only strong performers, regardless of their disability. Craig talks ▶

Craig Dearden-Phillips MBE

Craig Dearden-Phillips MBE is a social entrepreneur, author, speaker and ambassador for social business for the UK Government. Craig set up Speaking Up www.speakingup.org as a 24 year old to help people with disabilities to control their own lives. Fifteen years later, Speaking Up is now a £4.5 million business with multiple awards to its name.

Your Chance to Change the World: The No-fibbing Guide to Social Entrepreneurship by Craig Dearden-Phillips MBE is published by The Directory of Social Change

www.dsc.org.uk

about having a 'double bottom line' in which financial outcomes are measured as carefully as social ones.

The main difference between a true social enterprise and a regular entrepreneurial adventure is that all the profits are ploughed back into the business, forever. So if your ambition is to have a Ferrari and a big house, then social enterprise is not for you. Instead, insists Craig, "there is the sure fire knowledge that others' lives are better because of what your company has achieved".

The book cites a number of social entrepreneurs with similar, compelling motivation. Julie Stokes of Winston's Wish described "an overwhelming need that felt difficult to ignore." Owen Jarvis of Aspire Support UK says "it's the attraction of doing something new, setting your own course whilst doing things you feel passionately about."

So if 'giving back' appeals, but making a pile and leaving it to charity in your will seems too slow, maybe you should follow Craig Dearden-Phillips, become a social entrepreneur and 'give while you live'.

A Healthy Planet

Financial Times, 6th December 2008

As we approach the holiday season, there is the inevitable challenge of finding suitable Christmas gifts.

Perhaps I can help; many of the entrepreneurs that I meet have new and interesting Christmas gift ideas, including Shaylesh Patel and his company Healthy Planet.

Shaylesh had the traditional career route of first working for a big accounting firm then becoming the Financial Director of a growing company, in his case, in travel. But then he read a report that said that, for the first time in recent history, the life expectancy of his children was less than his own.

Seeing the connection between the way we lead our lives and its effect on our health and our planet, he formed Healthy Planet with a friend, an expert geographer.

Healthy Planet has a very simple premise. Through the website, you can adopt some land and everything on it in one of the 77,000 national parks around the world. Ninety percent of the money you provide goes straight to the land in question, and you can then choose which particular local sustainability project you wish to support.

For example, if you are concerned about the Amazonian rainforest you can cover the costs of a park ranger who will help prevent illegal logging in your chosen park. Patel has teamed up with Google Earth, so you can monitor your land directly and feel a real connection with the precise piece of real estate that you care about.

Healthy Planet is already a great success, with a wide range of customers. Individuals adopt land as gifts for themselves and their children; schools use the system for fundraising and creating geography, ICT and citizenship projects; large organisations use their Corporate Social Responsibility budgets to help save the planet in this very specific, efficient and personal way.

While it is a registered charity, it is also a bona-fide social enterprise. It is run like a proper business; for example, Patel and all the Healthy Planet team are measured solely on their performance like any good enterprise.

Healthy Planet and other similar organisations demonstrate an appropriate and realistic way forward out of the recession. Of course the blame for our current misfortune lies with the greedy and the stupid; capitalism as an economic system works better than any other, but no system is perfect and all models are prone to abuse. Hopefully the people in charge will set up better regulation in future, but I am not holding my breath.

Entrepreneurs are always busy thinking of ways to create wealth, and the big difference between this recession and the last one is that this time most of the young people who come to me for help are social entrepreneurs. Some like Patel are busy trying to save the planet or help people in the Third World directly. Others are building more traditional commercial ventures designed to make money, but also have one eye on helping those less fortunate than themselves, without detriment to their business.

> "You can monitor your land directly and feel a real connection with the precise piece of real estate that you care about"

The best Christmas present you can give someone this year is to provide encouragement that they should, after all, start that new business in the New Year.

Entrepreneurship does not have to involve your asking unpleasant people for money or putting your house on the line. In the first instance you should kick some ideas around with a friend who has the opposite set of skills to yourself. If you are good at starting things, they are good finishers, if you are introvert, they are extrovert; if you are bad with money, then they understand finance, and so on.

this is how **yoodoo** it.

You need to identify a problem and find people who trust you enough to take that problem away, and will also give you money for the privilege. If you can then deliver your product or service profitably, you have the basis for a business.

After that, the best advice I can give is to be three things: local, reliable and nice. People prefer to buy from someone close by, they want you to deliver valuable products and services and finally, to be easy to deal with.

If you follow these three simple rules, then you will be a successful entrepreneur; the rest, as they say, is detail.

Shaylesh Patel

A first generation British Asian and son of a businessman, former accountant and Finance Director Shaylesh Patel has used his network and prize-winning commercial experience to transform his interest in his children's welfare into a social enterprise and model like no other on the planet: Healthy Planet.

www.healthyplanet.org

Be Happy

Financial Times, 1st March 2008

So when was the last time you were really happy?

Most of us when asked that question would recall the birth of a child or watching a golden sunset on an idyllic holiday. I am sure most of you would not describe an episode from your working life.

Carmel McConnell has written an excellent book, The Happiness Plan: Simple Steps to a Happier Life, which unsurprisingly is selling like hot cakes.

She also has an interesting day-job, essentially going into large organisations to help them increase profits whilst at the same time increasing their social contribution. As both a former Greenham Common protester and a former senior executive at BT, she has an unusually wide perspective on society and its strengths and weaknesses.

Her process for achieving happiness is simple but effective. She first suggests that you should really understand the purpose of the organisation you work for, to get the big picture. What are you actually here to do?

This has to be something more relevant and personal than just 'to increase shareholder value'. What is it about your products and services of your company that brings joy to your customers, where you personally can make a difference?

Once you have worked this out, then you should find a way to be effective in a way which builds trust with people around you. Trust is a very simple premise; it means always doing what you say you are going to do.

Carmel finally recommends you try and understand what really makes you happy, urging everyone to ask themselves the question 'when and where am I happiest?' and then do more of whatever comes to mind. She observes that it is often when you help people to feel better about something, or even when they just say 'thank-you'.

this is how **yoodoo** it.

Entrepreneurs are the happiest people I meet. They are in control of their own destiny, can make a real difference and are working to increase their own shareholder value. But even the most successful entrepreneurs can feel unfulfilled without a sense of purpose over and above simply making money.

I always advise early stage entrepreneurs to put a social purpose to their business from day one; to find a way of helping people who need it, without detriment to their business. When they are successful, they can scale up this purpose, make a real difference to the world around them and feel better about themselves.

Money does not make you happy in itself, although I have observed that it does make misery more comfortable. But wealth does bring freedom, the ability to spend more time doing what you really enjoy, such as providing free mentoring for up-and-coming entrepreneurs.

Carmel McConnell

Carmel McConnell founded and leads food aid charity Magic Breakfast, which has delivered over a million free breakfasts to primary schools since 2002. It won Guardian Charity of the Year in 2005. She is a passionate public speaker on social change and business, and author of four books published by FT/Prentice Hall, including business bestseller Change Activist *and* The Happiness Plan. *She was voted UK Social Entrepreneur of the Year in 2008.*

www.magicbreakfast.com

The Happiness Plan: Simple Steps to a Happier Life is published by Prentice Hall.

Carmel McConnell's purpose is to use her management consulting and training to subsidise the charity she founded, called Magic Breakfast. Twenty-five percent of children in London go to school without breakfast, too hungry to learn.

She arranges free healthy breakfast deliveries to 32 London primary schools, then heads off to large organisations and teaches them vital business skills by getting them to work with the same kids. If you can work out how to motivate them, she reckons, you can then motivate anybody.

And maybe one day those same kids will remember you and ask for a job in your business. Keen and eager to learn, they will really enjoy doing all of those mundane jobs that you really hate, thus enabling you to spend more time with your family or on holiday, creating more happy memories.

Part Eleven:

Any Other Business

Most anthologies of newspaper columns have a section like this: odd, quirky pieces that don't really fit into any of the main categories.

I kick off with a piece on inspiration. Business, as I keep telling people, is supposed to be fun: 'Doing neat things with cool people.' Then I talk about The Beatles and Stackridge and discuss what we entrepreneurs can learn from what I consider to be the most creative team of all time. The Fab Four theme is then continued with a trip to Liverpool.

I then present a couple of pieces on doing business overseas, and then pay a visit to the inimitable WWE SmackDown!

To round the section off, I hand over to a true titan among inspirational gurus, L Vaughan Spencer, famous for (amongst other things) his 'Deep Tissue Ego Massage'.

Intrigued? Read on...

Be Inspired!

Financial Times, 22nd December 2007

Some people are very wary about going to see an inspirational speaker.

These are loud people, usually Americans, whose hair seems to be made out of Astroturf, their skin from Teflon and their teeth from ivory. They are people who shout a lot, are very rich and to most British people, very scary.

Yes, some inspirational speakers are more style than substance, but the best ones have tips, techniques and often complete life models, which can definitely help you and improve your life.

My first brush with a world-class inspirational speaker was a couple of years ago when I went to see Tony Robbins. Along with several thousand other people, I trooped down to the ExCel Centre, and was welcomed by eager volunteers, who high-fived me and assured me I was going to have a great day. On the stage itself, a group of higher-level enthusiasts in business suits were exuberantly disco dancing.

Finally Tony himself came on to tumultuous applause and did his thing, an expert blend of showmanship, good content, improvisation, and industrial-strength audience participation. This involved much 'call and response' with the audience. He suggested that if we agreed with what he said, we should say "yeah!" so we all did. He regularly asked us to finish his sentences, a classic way of getting people onto your wavelength.

I felt rather intimidated, though less by Robbins than by some members of the audience who seemed utterly galvanised but intensely needy. I left after a few hours, missing the opportunity to walk across hot coals and thus conquer any particular mental blocks I may have been experiencing at the time.

Last August I spent a whole day in the London Palladium at an event called Akasha, listening to four of the world's best inspirational speakers: Bob Procter ('tell me what you want and I will show you how to get it'), Roger Hamilton ('the key to wealth isn't in how you invest your money; it's in how you invest your time'), Gertrude Matshe ('your heart, your soul, your legacy') and Dr John Demartini ('you are never given a problem that you can't solve').

This was much more my cup of tea. I found them all superb performers with excellent content and much food for thought. For those of us that have been around the block a few times, input like this can help us put our experiences into perspective and add value to our own business and ethical models.

Afterwards, I spent some time with one of the speakers, John Demartini and I found him fascinating. He has had an amazing life, has studied extensively, and is genuinely determined to help as many people as he can achieve their potential.

> "I found them all superb performers with excellent content"

John was 17, a high school dropout, unable to read or write when he met a 93-year-old man called Paul Bragg who was able to catalyse a profound transformation by assisting him to awaken to an inspired vision of becoming a philosopher and a teacher.

He broke through his dyslexia and mastered reading and writing. He wrote his SATs and attained entry level into the University of Houston where he completed his Bachelor of Science degree in 1978.

He has spent a total of 36 years avidly researching over 260 different disciplines such as psychology, cosmology, economics, sociology, biology and theology.

He has many programmes including the Breakthrough Experience, a two-day program that challenges old assumptions about reality and offers you new formulas for living, relating to others and achieving your goals.

This uses his Demartini Method, which was derived from quantum physics and is a predetermined set of questions and actions that 'neutralise your emotional charges and brings balance to your mind and body'. Dr John Demartini is a genuinely very interesting man — I thoroughly recommend going to one of his talks.

All motivational speakers offer a free talk first, and then try and sell you a more expensive follow-on — but if you feel nervous about this, you can always leave your credit cards and chequebook at home. And, yes, there will be people there who seem to be rather scary 'inspiration addicts'. But you will get to see one of the world's top speakers at close range. And it might even change your life..

Dr John Demartini

Dr John Demartini is a human behavioural specialist, educator, author and founder of the Demartini Institute, a private research and education institute with a focus on empowering individuals and organisations and transforming micro and macro social dynamics.

Dr Demartini has written over 40 books and been a featured guest on CNN's Larry King Live. He speaks 300 days per year and has shared the stage with noted speakers such as Steven Covey, Donald Trump and Deepak Chopra.

www.drdemartini.com

Something About The Beatles (and Stackridge)

Financial Times, 7th June 2008

I am often asked what I think about the
television show Dragon's Den.

While it has done a sterling job in raising awareness of
entrepreneurship in the UK, particularly amongst young people, it
has to be remembered that it is only a television show.

You could argue that it has as much to with day-to-day
entrepreneurship as The X-Factor has to do with The Beatles.
But after further consideration of this analogy, I realised that
The Beatles themselves were entrepreneurs, and followed the
Beermat model.

They developed an elevator pitch ('like Elvis, Little Richard and
Chuck Berry, only local'), found a mentor (their manager Brian
Epstein), and then a first customer (producer George Martin, who
signed them to EMI).

They had plenty of upsets and rejections along the way,
including being famously turned down by Dick Rowe at Decca, who
famously said that 'guitar bands are on the way out'.

But eventually The Beatles were at the right place at the right
time, specifically The Ed Sullivan Show on February 9th 1964, when
Paul McCartney counted in All My Loving and 73 million people
simultaneously got the point.

There was inevitably competition, for example in the shape
of The Beach Boys' stunning Pet Sounds, but they immediately
innovated clear of the pack with Sergeant Pepper's Lonely Hearts
Club Band.

They were then at the peak of their powers, delivering probably
the best double A-side of all time, Strawberry Fields Forever/Penny
Lane. Ironically, this was the first Beatles single for 5 years not to go

to number one, beaten to the top slot by Release Me by Engelbert Humperdinck: proof that the customer is not always right...

That year, 1967, also saw them release the best song ever written about entrepreneurship, All You Need Is Love. What entrepreneur could argue with the opening line: "There's nothing you can do that can't be done"?

> "The best song ever written about entrepreneurship is All You Need Is Love"

But in August 1967, the Beatles had another critical moment; their manager Brian Epstein died of a suspected accidental drug overdose. The Beatles decided they could manage themselves, but their next project, Magical Mystery Tour, while containing fabulous music, was a critical flop, a self-indulgent film which did not really work on black and white TV, the only multimedia platform available in most homes that Boxing Day.

Then came their next album, The Beatles, now known as The White Album, which again featured great songs, but was a less than pleasant experience for them, with Ringo Starr quitting at one point.

George Martin became exasperated by the lack of teamwork — sometimes they would work separately in three different studios — and, disappointed by the final result, resolved not to work with them again.

The next Beatles project, which eventually became the album Let It Be, was another difficult experience, and was shelved. But they decided to come together with George Martin again for one last album, Abbey Road, which he described as a very happy album to produce.

The Beatles story has many business learning points, and is now my keynote presentation for both entrepreneurs and large organisations. It goes down particularly well in schools and colleges, which gives me great hope for the future of UK plc.

SOMETHING ABOUT

THE BEATLES

Illustration by Ayd Instone, www.aydinstone.com

My talk is called Something about the Beatles, the title of a song by my second favourite band, Stackridge. Their career in the 70s attempted to replicate much of the Beatles model: they were a popular live act, were produced by George Martin, and even played at a national stadium (Wembley, rather than Shea). But they did not sell millions of records, and eventually split up.

However, the Stackridge story has a happy ending; two of the members, James Warren and Andy Davis, later formed The Korgis and had a huge international hit with Everybody's Got To Learn Sometime. Stackridge have now reformed, are touring again, and have just released an excellent new album, A Victory For Common Sense.

I met with them at their recent 100 Club gig in London, and they seemed serene and radiant. They felt they had made a success of their lives — a useful reminder to all entrepreneurs that you don't have to amass vast wealth to create a successful business with happy staff, happy customers and enough money to go around.

As The Beatles themselves said on Abbey Road, "And in the end the love you take is equal to the love you make."

Stackridge can be found at www.stackridge.net

Liverpool Vision

Financial Times, 17th July 2009

It is good to recharge your 'spirit battery' now and then.

I always feel enriched when visiting Westminster Abbey. Recently, however, I returned from a pilgrimage to my first spiritual home, Liverpool.

I have always had a deep affection for the area; my first job after leaving university was as a construction engineer, based in Widnes. It was always a thrill to sit on the town's station platform (where Paul Simon wrote Homeward Bound) and to take the short trip to the hallowed stomping grounds of my great musical heroes, The Beatles.

What really struck me then about Liverpool was not so much the place itself as the people. They were uniformly open and hugely welcoming to a stranger in their midst, despite my being a slightly confused ex-public schoolboy, ostensibly from the better side of the tracks.

In the 1980s, Liverpool went through a period of trauma. The Toxteth riots were followed by the Hillsborough disaster, which left a sad legacy and still results in lingering prejudices from outsiders. Now, however, it is completely transformed and almost unrecognisable from those dark days.

The city is well laid-out, airy and clean; it has carefully preserved the best of its heritage while simultaneously developing new attractions, such as the Liverpool One shopping centre, which connects the city centre to the formerly grim Pier Head waterfront area. But the chief asset of the city still remains the people who live and work there.

Sir Paul McCartney explains the nature and attraction of the region perfectly in the documentary The Beatles Anthology. Liverpool covers a relatively small area, about ten square miles, but has its own distinct dialect and culture as well as a deep sense of civic pride. Every taxi driver is an ambassador for the city; most people you meet serving in hotels and bars are locals and fiercely proud of their home.

Getting to Liverpool has greatly improved since my first trips there. It may be popular to criticise Virgin Trains, but my train was clean and well appointed, the journey time only just over 2 hours, and my off-peak return tickets booked online cost only £35.

I felt compelled to book into The Hard Day's Night Hotel. Its Beatles theme isn't tacky: it's a delightful boutique hotel, reminiscent of the Hotel du Vin and Malmaison chains. It has a perfect location for Beatles' enthusiasts, on the corner of Mathew Street, home to the now rebuilt Cavern Club.

> "The chief asset of the city still remains the people who live and work there"

While tourism is important to Liverpool, to get a wider business perspective on the region, I visited Liverpool Vision, the city's economic development company. They are charged with leading the next phase of economic development.

The fruits of the £4bn or so of the mostly private investment include the expansion of Liverpool John Lennon, now the UK's fastest growing regional airport, ACC Liverpool which houses the BT Convention Centre, and the Echo Arena, capable of seating over 10,000 concert goers.

The city is home to an increasing number of pharmaceuticals and biotechnology companies, such as Eli Lily, Novartis and Astra Zeneca, who have access to leading-edge life sciences research and development in local universities.

Other recent inward investors include shipping giant Maersk (headquarters relocation), Prinovis, who invested in a £130m gravure printing plant in Speke to produce large volumes of high-quality publications and catalogues, and stockbroker Panmure Gordon, who recently opened their first regional office at Rumford

Investments in Chapel Street, near where Beatles manager Brian Epstein once had his NEMS record store.

Liverpool Vision is particularly focused on attracting the creative and media industries.

I promised to return to Liverpool and to counter any lingering doubts about its merits by writing about its new generation of very successful entrepreneurs. If you are looking to relocate your business to a thriving and optimistic city, with a family atmosphere and highly skilled local work force, Liverpool has to be high on your list.

Of course, any business decision should be based on compelling benefits, carefully considered. My suggestion would be to present the business logic first, and then play your hard-nosed decision makers the Beatles tracks In My Life, Strawberry Fields Forever and Penny Lane.

If they don't get it then, they never will. ▪

Image: Liverpool Vision/McCoy Wynne Photography

Liverpool Vision is the city's economic development company

www.liverpoolvision.co.uk

Welcome to Estonia!

Financial Times, 27th December 2008

Here's a radical suggestion to make the best of the current tough times: why not move to Estonia?

I was there recently to explain to them how to cope with the current recession. Last time we in the UK went through one in 1991, Estonians were rather preoccupied with becoming independent from the Soviet Union. At the time, many expected the worst; they had seen both German and Soviet tanks in recent history. But they came through the process as a new, young country, keen to share their own skills with the outside world.

One thing they decided to do early on was to make the most of the new internet technology. It helped not having archaic legacy systems: Estonia resolved to make itself an e-country and put everything on the web.

Today, Estonians have an entirely connected country, with a completely transparent legislature and everyone happy to submit their tax returns on-line. Identity cards were seamlessly introduced; it obviously helped to have a population used to a high level of surveillance, but the main driver in their swift adoption was making the identity cards also work on the public transport system.

Mobile phones are used for almost everything, including a simple public parking system, now being taken up by local authorities around the world. It will soon be used for voting in elections. Estonia's dynamic business environment has been able to catalyse several well-known international successes, including Skype, the internet-based voice service.

Generally, Estonia is doing better in the recession than most countries. It has suffered an inevitable slump in property prices, arguably an expected consequence of the previous unsustainable boom. Many people have lost money, but the wise ones are just biding their time, waiting for the market to recover; after all, there is only a finite amount of space in the country, as in the UK.

Of course, Estonia is only a very small country with around 1.3 million people, and so does not represent a very big market for the major players. But Estonia's small size also provides one important advantage. You can get things done.

I had a very agreeable chat over a beer with Estonia's president, Toomas Hendrik Ilves. Charming and relaxed, he explained that Estonia had fared better in the recent crisis as their banks are owned by Swedish and Finnish institutions, which suffered back in 1991 and have consequently been much more circumspect and risk-averse since.

He gave me details of their low fixed rate of corporation tax and 100% relief for companies that re-invest. He suggested that more people from the UK might want to base their companies in Estonia, easy to do as the country is a member of the European Union.

You may recall a recent news item detailing how our National Health Service has fallen down the league table below Estonia. You may also have read items that express concern over the costs and problems associated with the twelve billion pound patient record system currently under development.

I met an Estonian doctor, Madis Tiik, who had been looking at the same challenge in his country. Lacking any detailed understanding of complex project management, and oblivious to suggestions that it was impossible to implement, he just got on and did it. The system is being rolled out next year.

"Oblivious to suggestions that it was impossible to implement, he just got on and did it"

I understand that the UK database is much larger. But I also observe that entrepreneur-driven businesses based on huge databases such as Friends Reunited and Facebook seem to be managing quite well, using simple standards and XML: you can put anything in a web browser.

Perhaps this is why many successful entrepreneurs move to islands or other small countries. They remember the tribal atmosphere of the early days of their start-up, when if they said something it got done. Having status in a small community can make things happen quickly, as long as you know the right people. The bigger the country, the more silly rules there tend to be.

If this is the case, then would you not prefer to be in a small country like Estonia, where you can get things done quickly, and more importantly, make a real difference? ▪

The Republic of Estonia is situated in the Baltic region of Northern Europe, bordered to the north by the Gulf of Finland, to the west by the Baltic Sea, to the south by Latvia, and to the east by the Russian Federation. It has around 1.3 million people and one of the best telecommunications infrastructures in the world. It is a member of the United Nations, the European Community and NATO.

Foreign Policy

Financial Times, 17th January 2009

Every cloud has a silver lining; the current run
on the pound means it is much easier to sell our
services abroad.

The main problem is that 'abroad' is a very strange place
populated by foreigners, many of whom are very different to us
and have some idiosyncratic ways of doing business.

For example, I had to understand before I went on a recent
speaking tour that the three Baltic states are three very dissimilar
places, as different as Germany, Spain and the UK. Lithuania is a
county with strong historical connections to Poland, while Estonia
is more like Finland. Latvia, in the middle, has a troubled but
strong link to Russia.

"In the Far East, to
put oneself first is
seen as immature"

I needed to learn more, so I met with
Dr Debbie Swallow from 4C International.
Debbie studied Spanish and worked as a
translator, but later applied for a job with
a consultancy company based in Finland.

At her interview for this, she was bemused by the lack of
questions and thus rather surprised to be offered the position.
It was later explained to her that Finnish people do not ask
questions; they assume that if you have important information, it
will be included in the presentation.

Debbie now gives specialist advice on cross-cultural issues. For
British people she wrote a book on Finnish customs and etiquette
called Culture Shock! Finland. For Finns who want to do business
abroad, she wrote Make More Sales with Better Presentations,
looking at the cultural hurdles they might face, including the issue
that most Finns are suspicious of people who talk too much. This
can be quite a hurdle for salespeople and professional speakers.

In Estonia, I took Debbie's advice and started my presentation
by asking the audience questions. This went down well: once I

had listened to them a bit, they were prepared to listen to my talk.

A key difference between cultures is the question of the relative stress placed on the individual or the organisation. In Anglo-Saxon cultures, the individual is most important, and business is typically arranged around the need to provide controls against bad behaviour, using lawyers and contracts.

In the Far East, to put oneself first is seen as immature; the needs of the group are paramount and reputation is everything. Debbie gives the example of a British speaker asking a Singaporean audience if anyone had made a particular mistake in business.

There was complete silence; no one wanted to admit to weakness. When the speaker changed the language slightly to ask, "who has made a particular mistake in business, like me", the audience warmed to the concept of a collective learning experience and didn't want the speaker, now one of them, to lose face.

Dr Debbie Swallow

Dr Debbie Swallow works with entrepreneurs both at home and abroad to expand their businesses into foreign markets. She brings a locally-specific understanding of markets and people to international deals so you can gain early successes, increase profits and make quicker returns on your international trading.

www.4Cinternational.com

My own business history is littered with cultural blunders. I once received a fax from Japan inquiring about running a seminar. I told them the price and booked my flights, looking forward to a week's holiday in Tokyo. The next day, a 20-page fax of questions arrived. I spent most of the night answering the questions in great detail. The next day another 20-page fax of new questions arrived.

By the time I got to Tokyo, I had clearly demonstrated my immaturity and ignorance, especially when confronted with teams of negotiators who all said 'yes' to everything but then proceeded to re-negotiate everything the next day, from scratch. By the end of the week I had given everything away. I now know to ask for expert advice and in-depth local support before getting on a plane.

On a more upbeat note, Debbie recently worked in Malawi where they have no concept of win:lose — they are only familiar with win:win. Their way of business is to give as much as they can up-front, expecting reciprocation, a technique which I have personally observed works very well, especially in social entrepreneurship.

Wrestling with Content

Financial Times, Saturday 22nd November 2008

Like many people I dream that one day I will have my own television show.

This is not completely unrealistic. Journalists and TV researchers looking for input to their articles and programmes already call me up. Recent career highlights include an appearance on BBC Breakfast and auditioning for a prime-time quiz show. Sadly, I did not get selected for the latter; perhaps I was not 'edgy' enough. But a career in sales has made me impervious to rejection and thus even more determined.

If all else fails, I can always make my own programme. It is now relatively inexpensive to generate your own content and post it on the internet. Many people have done this and gone on to great commercial success. The challenge is getting people first to notice your content, and then, crucially, to pay money for it.

"The perfect matching of content with a deep understanding of how to monetise the various channels to the consumer"

To understand how to do this I went to see a subject matter expert, Andrew Whitaker. His university degree was History and Political Science but he was always drawn to working in television. He started on the lowest rung at NBC doing studio tours, eventually working on some great shows, including Late Night with David Letterman and Saturday Night Live.

This was the perfect apprenticeship, enabling him to decide which particular aspect of television interested him most. He was attracted to a career in sales but NBC could not offer him the right opportunities, so he approached Titan Sports, the parent company of what eventually became World Wrestling Entertainment (WWE).

His first TV job was in television syndication, helping to persuade local channels to take WWE output. He was then involved in the early days of pay-per-view and is now responsible for television, digital, live events and licensing sales as President of Europe, the Middle East and Africa. Today WWE television programming can be seen in more than 130 countries and each year more than 7,500 hours of programming is broadcast in 23 languages all over the world.

I am sure I am not betraying any trade secrets when I explain that WWE is not exactly a competitive Olympic sport. Whitaker describes it neatly as an 'Action Soap Opera'. The characters are selected very carefully and then perform in some very sophisticated pieces of theatre, which follow simple but multi-layered narrative themes. It is much more complex than a simple battle of good versus evil, otherwise the audiences would soon tire of the spectacle.

What is interesting about WWE from a business perspective is the perfect matching of content with a deep understanding of how to monetise the various channels to the consumer.

WWE is essentially just one property, but is delivered on many different platforms, including retail, live events, home entertainment, video games, pay-per-view and both free-to-air and subscription TV. Each platform feeds and cross-pollinates each other, and the skill is in constantly playing with the various business models, seeing what works and adapting accordingly.

Many entrepreneurs I meet are content-oriented, with a great idea for some engaging video or audio. I explain that they must also have someone on the team who understands precisely who would want to pay for this content and the channels they would use to access it.

Television commissioning editors and Hollywood studios claim to have this all worked out, but I am always reminded of the famous quote by William Goldman, scriptwriter of Butch Cassidy and the Sundance Kid. He was asked how one can tell if a particular script will make a great movie. He replied: "In Hollywood, nobody knows anything". So your crazy idea for content might not be crazy after all.

My personal quest for knowledge led me to the showpiece of the WWE property, the WWE SmackDown live event at the O2 Arena. Undertaker, Triple H, Big Show, Vladimir Kozlov, The Great Khali, Michelle McCool and many others entered the ring to their own specific theme music and deafening firework displays. The Good Guys suffered near total physical collapse due to the terrible punishment they received, but somehow managed to recover just in time to defeat their enemies.

I completely loved it: the whole crazy spectacle and the consummate skill of some very big people throwing themselves around with abandon, but without injuring themselves or any members of the audience. The place was completely packed and we all left happy.

So now I know exactly how I'm going to get onto TV! I'm off to the gym. I may be some time...

Andrew Whitaker

In his role of President, International, Andrew Whitaker leads WWE's global expansion. Andrew assumed this role in November 2007 after spearheading WWE's international television business for 10 years, negotiating the largest international television contracts in WWE's history.

Andrew joined WWE in 1987 to work on domestic television syndication and develop its pay-per-view business. He commenced his career at NBC, working on NBC News, Late Night with David Letterman, The Today Show, Saturday Night Live and The Cosby Show.

World Wrestling Entertainment can be found at www.wwe.com

Don't Be Needy, Be Succeedy

Financial Times, 8th November 2008

We all need inspiration and good business advice in these hard times.

So I have been combing bookstores for leading-edge thought leadership from the great business experts. Many of the most popular books seem to originate in the USA. But isn't that the place that's the source for our current misfortunes?

Never fear! At last, I have found a book by a British motivational guru, L Vaughan Spencer: Don't Be Needy, Be Succeedy, The A to Zee of Motivitality.

Spencer made his fortune in the refrigerated transport business, and is now Business Ambassador for the South East England Tree Fellowship and Acme Products Ltd Visiting Professor of Succeedership at the University of the Isle of Wight.

His list of published books is very impressive and includes seminal works such as Chicken Nuggets for the Soul, The Seven Hobbies of Highly Effective People and Who Moved My Cheeseburger? Strangely, I could not find any listings for these on Amazon, so called the number on his website, the 'Succeeder Hotline'.

I had a conversation with a member of his staff, who explained that the lack of availability of many of his published books was the result of a conspiracy by a number of people, including a rival motivational speaker. It was a long and interesting story. A few months later, I discovered that the hotline was in fact a premium rate number and the call had cost me several hundred pounds.

I sent an e-mail to complain, and eventually received an answer from the great man himself, saying that legally I had agreed to a 'Virtual Vaughan Session' and I was at fault for not sending him a photo of myself and buying another book for a friend, which was apparently all part of the process of learning how to succeed.

this is how **yoodoo** it.

The conversation became quite heated, so he offered to convert my payment into a free place on his Business Boot Camp. He also said that anger is 'vital in today's FMBE (Fast Moving Business Environment)', and explained that the Boot Camp would be a perfect place for me to express my pent-up anger and channel it into business success.

The day started with Moisturiser, which Spencer explains is 'vital in today's FMBE (Fast Moving Business Environment)', quoting ancient French Canadian wisdom, which translated as: 'Man with dry face no win big deal.' When I pointed out that many women are very successful in business, he claimed that this proved his point and directed me to his own range of skincare products.

> "Anger is vital in today's fast moving business environment"

The next part of the program was called 'Movement and Dance', which involved us moving around to very loud 70s disco music, with Spencer himself encouraging the female members of the workshop to loosen any constricting items of clothing.

I was beginning to become suspicious, as the rest of the agenda for the workshop included 'Urban Tribal Drumming', a 2-hour case study on how Spencer changed the face of refrigerated transport, and 'Deep Tissue Ego Massage' by someone called Cranston and his team of former paramilitaries...

L Vaughan Spencer is, of course, a spoof, the creation of Neil Mullarkey, one of the founders of The Comedy Store Players. But like all good satire, his barbs are unnervingly close to the mark, especially for people like me whose day job involves inspiring audiences.

It is very easy to be cynical about the neo-religious fervour stirred up by motivational speakers; a friend of mine once referred to their events as 'hope for the hopeless'. It is certainly true that some people spend money they cannot afford on 'get rich' programmes, which succeed only in increasing the wealth of the speaker, rather than the audience.

But on balance, I am in favour of anything that lifts the spirit. For every sceptic there are many more people who do get real value from the programs, otherwise the genuine L Vaughan Spencers would have been put out of business years ago.

My recommendation is not to follow their models slavishly, but to use them to add perspective to your own experience, and hopefully learn from your mistakes and build on your successes. All the motivational speakers have the same basic themes: you need to take personal responsibility for your own situation rather than blaming others; you should take action rather than prevaricate.

It is also important to retain your sense of humour. As L Vaughan Spencer himself says: "Successful business is not about talk-talk. My book is all do-do."

L Vaughan Spencer

L Vaughan Spencer returned to his native Britain after a lengthy sojourn in Canada where he built a huge following and massive reputation as a personal growth guru. In 2004, he was named Business Speaker of the Year for Bedfordshire and Hertfordshire and came 12th in the Northern Hemisphere Motivator of the Year (Under-40 Middleweight Section).

He is the chief executive of the L Vaughan Spencer Foundation, a not-for-much-profit organisation dedicated to its betterment and of Succeeder Solutions who provide 'bespoke solutions to tricky problems'.

Don't Be Needy, Be Succeedy, the A to Zee of Motivality by L Vaughan Spencer is published by Profile Books. (I mean this one!)

this is how **yoodoo** it.

Neil Mullarkey

*Neil Mullarkey founded Britain's
top improvisation troupe, The
Comedy Store Players, in 1985.
Credits include Austin Powers
movies (International Man of
Mystery and Goldmember), Whose
Line Is it Anyway, I'm Sorry I
Haven't A Clue, QI and Have I Got
News For You.*

www.neilmullarkey.com

Part Twelve:

Memos to Number 10...

I can't resist closing with a trio of pieces on politics.

I really do believe that entrepreneurs create a lot more social change than politicians — but supposing the two disciplines actually merged?

People often describe politics as 'the lunatics taking over the asylum'. What if the asylum were taken over by the staff, the people who actually made it work?

And the book closes with a very recent column, my final message: 'All You Need Is Gumption' — true for entrepreneurs and government alike.

'Do Nothing' Government

Financial Times, 7th February 2009

I always enjoy the political programme Question Time.

A recent programme involved the Opposition accusing the Government of being responsible for our current economic woes, and the PM accusing the opposition of being the 'do nothing' party.

But the more I hear this second accusation, the more I wonder if it is really an accusation at all. Couldn't doing nothing be something of vote-winner? Entrepreneurs certainly want the government to 'do nothing', or rather to leave us alone.

Sooner or later the banks will start lending freely again, either forced by their new masters, or if still privately owned, in response to market demand. Those of us who know how to use debt sensibly are ready to use this to create growth in the economy.

The main thing holding us back is the excessive regulation we face as soon as we put our heads above the parapet. Employment regulations are complicated and punitive. My e-mailbox is full of complaints from people with business premises, complaining about visits from representatives from their local authority threatening them with punitive fines on what they consider to be spurious health and safety or environmental grounds. (To add insult to injury, they notice that all these busy-bodies are on fat salaries and index-linked pensions.)

A second disincentive from government is the level of specific business taxation, such as business rates, and the National Insurance surcharges we face the moment we do what the government wants us to do, which is to start employing people.

Income tax, which the media make such a ballyhoo about, is much less of an issue: we want the chance to earn the money, fair and square, after which many of us are happy to pay a reasonable level of income tax, as long as corporate and government employees face the same regime. We understand that schools, police, defence, roads, hospitals etc aren't provided by Santa Claus.

this is how **yoodoo** it.

We would love to see the UK designated as an Enterprise Zone, with no taxation or bureaucracy at all for start-up and small companies with a turnover under £100,000 and fewer than six full-time employees. We would love to see all the irritating regulations for business and enterprise reformed away forever by the Department of Business Enterprise and Regulatory Reform, now remodelled as the BIS.

While we are waiting, entrepreneurs are doing what we do best, which is finding clever and legal ways around the system. Many of us now run 'virtual' companies, using self-employed experts who come and go as required with minimal employment bureaucracy.

If we need help, we tend to talk to other entrepreneurs, rather than to government.

Government bodies set up to help business seem to vary wildly in the quality of the service they provide. Some are truly excellent, but others...

> "We would love to see the UK designated as an Enterprise Zone"

My advice to the government-backed entities that support entrepreneurs is to do rather little. There should be free events to inspire and encourage the 18 million people that surveys show are interested in starting a business to take that first step, operating a cash model in the early days.

As their businesses gain traction, there should be free networking events where they can meet other entrepreneurs for advice on how to grow. Help should also be provided in dealing with bureaucracy and form-filling, including securing government loans and grants where available.

I'm not a conspiracy theorist, and actually believe that governments usually mean well. But being used only to spending other people's money, government has no idea how to appeal to those who generate it for a living. We entrepreneurs are highly motivated, and keen to create wealth for our country and ourselves. We would just like our government to let us get on with it.

Building a Better Britain

Financial Times, 2nd May 2009

There was a recent announcement of a planned new income tax rate of 50% for those earning over £150,000.

This was followed by reports that some people, including some well-known entrepreneurs, were planning on leaving the UK.

I was angrier with the latter than the former. The 50% rate idea is clearly flawed, so will not last long; the Chancellor swiftly hinted that it might be dispensed with once things pick up a bit.

What I found really disappointing was that some entrepreneurs revealed why they are in business; not for the thrill of being their own boss or the joy of making a difference to their staff, customers, industry or even planet. These entrepreneurs are only in it to make money for themselves, and they always think they need more.

The big question is, why? Are they unable to calculate how many boats they can actually water- ski behind? They are also unconcerned that they are generally despised for not having any kind of moral compass; especially as they are already surrounded by tax experts, so pay much less than the 'little people', anyway.

What goes around comes around, and their fate will be to uproot their family and live in miserable tax-exile status with other bitter people who put greed before happiness. Stackridge have a great song about this, The Old Country, on their new album A Victory for Common Sense.

I work almost exclusively with early stage entrepreneurs who dream of one day earning as much as £150,000 per year. By then, they will have a company of perhaps 20 people whom they love and a client list of good friends. This successful 'boutique business' will enable them to live the life they want, with children at private school (if that is their wish), a very small mortgage, a nice car and the ability to take two good well-deserved holidays a year.

They are unconcerned about the 50% tax rate — but are eagerly hoping for real government support of the only people who are going to get us out of this mess: the UK's entrepreneurs. 'Real support' means a radical sweeping away of pointless laws and regulations, and a fairer deal on tax.

My budget policy would have been to completely abolish all taxation and all but the most basic regulation for companies with less than five employees or a turnover under £100,000.

> "'Real support' means a radical sweeping away of pointless laws and regulations"

This would provide the most fundamental and instant kick-start to the economy in recent times. It would attract foreign investment at astronomical rates. It would change the emphasis of our economy to entrepreneurship at a single stroke. It would also be tremendous fun for everyone concerned, both the companies and their customers.

The alternative is not good. If something doesn't turn up for the Chancellor, then we will receive the fateful knock on the door from the International Monetary Fund. They will undoubtedly insist on a change in policy, cutting public spending by 10%, and then another 10%, and so on, on a regular basis, until they think they stand a realistic chance of getting their money back.

This is bad news for those in sinecure state jobs on index-linked pensions, who will undoubtedly be the first to go. This would be a good thing — but the government might then try and cut back on people who actually provide the rest of us with a service, such as nurses and street cleaners.

Genuine unrest will follow. The rumble of the tumbrel wagon is not far away: as the protests against the G20 summit showed, there are plenty of well-educated, middle-class would-be Robespierres out there, which is the only thing a government is truly afraid of.

My advice to government is that if you want a practical 'last throw of the die' you should set us entrepreneurs free to rebuild UK plc. We would do this in our own style, and not that of failed bankers, would-be tax exiles or faceless bureaucrats.

This isn't as crazy as it might sound. If any politicians actually did this, we would definitely vote for them. And 'we' are a lot of people. We estimate there are over 18 million would-be entrepreneurs in the UK, and we all have votes.

All You Need Is Gumption

Financial Times, 26th September 2010

In my experience, entrepreneurs tend to fall into two categories.

Some are attracted by the opportunity of starting their own business but are later unable or unwilling to actually make it happen. Others have 'gumption', defined as initiative, resourcefulness and courage, all typical attributes of the successful entrepreneur.

I first met Mark Prisk at an event several years ago when he was Shadow Minister for Small Business. As a former entrepreneur, he clearly understood the issues we face and at the time said all the right things about reducing red tape and encouraging enterprise.

> "For that amount of money a halfway decent entrepreneur could have built another eBay or Facebook"

I was pleased to note that within the first 100 days of his taking office in the new administration as Minister for Business and Enterprise the government had the gumption to overhaul the Regional Development Agencies and Business Links.

Few entrepreneurs have mourned the passing of these government agencies, considering them to be overly bureaucratic and largely filled with people unqualified to provide advice to entrepreneurs. There has also been considerable anger about the revelation that the Business Link web site had cost £105 million over 3 years. For that amount of money a halfway decent entrepreneur could have built another eBay or Facebook.

The new government strategy is the formation of Local Enterprise Partnerships (LEPs). Prisk explained to me that he felt that entrepreneurs would be best served by people in their local area, and they should decide on their own geographical remit, rather than have it imposed on them by central government.

The first 57 proposals for LEPs have been received and the list of applicants makes very interesting reading. I was fascinated to learn that Aylesbury Vale had decided to partner with Milton Keynes, Central Bedfordshire, Luton, Northampton Borough, Bicester, Banbury, Daventry, Corby and others to form a South East Midlands LEP.

Andrew Grant, Chief Executive of Aylesbury Vale District Council explained to me that they had more to gain by being aligned with these partners rather than grouped into the South East region, as they were under the old structure. They are also delighted to have been chosen to be the new headquarters of Peter Jones' National Enterprise Academy (NEA).

Another local authority showing similar gumption is Sheffield City Council. Chief Executive John Mothersole told me that, like entrepreneurship itself, it was all about having the confidence to make the very first step. Forming the LEP was an easy decision, and that they had already set the wheels in motion to establish Sheffield as one of the UK's prime locations for entrepreneurs by running the MADE Festival earlier this month.

The MADE Festival featured the official launch of the third NEA in Sheffield College's purpose-built new building, a keynote presentation from Wilfred Emmanuel-Jones, The Black Farmer, Rachel Bridge explaining how to make a million before lunch, and a two-day workshop by Doug Richard showing how to build a web-based business from scratch.

The MADE Festival was sufficiently high profile to attract not only Mark Prisk, but also Secretary of State for Business, Innovation and Skills, Vince Cable. He told me that the LEPs would be a key element of the government's plans to encourage the UK's entrepreneurs to innovate the country out of the recession.

this is how **yoodoo** it.

The submissions for LEPs will be evaluated and their activities monitored over the coming months, against a backdrop of little or no central government financial support in the short term.

My guess is that local authorities like Aylesbury Vale and Sheffield who mirror the style of their own successful entrepreneurs and show the most gumption, will be the ones to benefit most from government largesse in the future.

About Yoodoo.Biz

If these stories have inspired you, then Yoodoo.biz should be your next destination.

Yoodoo.biz is a free web site, designed specifically for people thinking of starting a business, even if you are not sure if you can do it.

It contains videos and quizzes and features over 80 subject matter experts, including several of the people featured in this book.

Yoodoo guides you through the whole process, including helping you build a plan for your business!

You can find the site here:
www.yoodoo.biz

About Ecademy Press

Ecademy Press is an independent publisher founded in 2005. The company specialises in high quality business books and personal development books that truly help people grow and develop. Our philosophy is based on 'winning by sharing', and with our model everybody wins: the author, the publisher and, most importantly, the reader. To date, we have published over 100 books.

The company only prints books as needed, commonly called 'print-on-demand'. We have printed as few as one or two books at a time, and we have on occasion printed runs of thousands of books, but only to fulfil orders. This is in keeping with our concern for the environment and our commitment to eliminate the traditional publishing practice of remaindering books. We also publish many formats of ebook.

We are constantly looking for ways to partner with talented authors to bring great books into the market and raise the profile of our authors. Many of our authors receive excellent media coverage and feature in the top ten books of their category on Amazon. We also see our books being stocked in more and more bookstores and online retailers around the world.

If you would like to know more about publishing with Ecademy Press, please feel free to browse our website:

www.ecademy-press.com.

ecademyPRESS
www.ecademy-press.com

We hope you have enjoyed this book and look forward to engaging with you again in the near future.

About the Author

Mike Southon was educated at Papplewick School, Ascot, and Wellington College in Crowthorne.

He only lasted one year at Imperial College, preferring to drink beer and chase women rather than go to lectures.

He then had a variety of jobs, including helping British Leyland assemble trucks and buses and making sugar into detergent, before just about completing a degree in Chemical Engineering and Management Economics at the University of Bradford.

It was there, in 1984, that he met Mike Banahan and Andy Rutter, who, along with Peter and David Griffiths were founders of The Instruction Set. He joined them as Director of Sales and Marketing, and the five of them built the company to one that employed 150 people and was sold to Hoskyns Group in 1989.

Mike then set off in a different direction, pursuing a full-time, and very successful, performing career in colleges and theatres as 70s disco legend Mike Fab-Gere. Then he went back into the business world, working on 17 start-ups, some of which later went public, others of which went broke. "The latter were as informative as the former," he comments.

All these experiences went into creating The Beermat Entrepreneur, which was published in 2002, and later The Boardroom Entrepreneur and Sales on a Beermat, all co-authored with Chris West.

Mike is now one of the world's top business speakers and conference moderators, a Fellow of the Professional Speakers Association. He appears all over the world, from events in schools to major international conferences.

When not speaking live, he provides free mentoring to entrepreneurs.

He also writes a column, My Business, in the *Financial Times* every weekend.

Mike can be contacted at mike@beermat.biz

www.mikesouthon.com

www.ft.com/mikesouthon

Lightning Source UK Ltd.
Milton Keynes UK
20 November 2010

163150UK00001B/18/P